Decorating Sweaters with Duplicate Stitch

Decorating Sweaters with Duplicate Stitch

60 Gorgeous Designs
··
One Easy Embroidery Technique

Nola Theiss

A STERLING/LARK BOOK
Sterling Publishing Co. Inc.   New York

Editor: Deborah Morgenthal
Art Director: Kathleen Holmes
Production: Elaine Thompson
English Translation: Networks, Inc.

Library of Congress Cataloging-in-Publication Data
Theiss, Nola.
    Decorating sweaters with duplicate stitch : 60 gorgeous
designs / one easy embroidery technique / Nola Theiss.
    "A Sterling/Lark book."
    Includes index.
    ISBN 0-8069-0810-6
    1. Embroidery--Patterns.   2. Sweaters.   I. Title.
TT775.T48   1994
746.9'2--dc20   94-7980
                                                          CIP

10 9 8 7 6 5 4 3 2 1

A Sterling/Lark Book

Published in 1994 by Sterling Publishing Co., Inc.
387 Park Avenue South, New York, NY 10016

Produced by Altamont Press, Inc.
50 College Street, Asheville, NC 28801

Distributed in Canada by Sterling Publishing
   c/o Canadian Manda Group, P.O. Box 920, Station U
   Toronto, Ontario, Canada M8Z 5P9
Distributed in the United Kingdom by Cassell PLC
   Villiers House, 41/47 Strand, London WC2N 5JE, England
Distributed in Australia by Capricorn Link (Australia) Pty Ltd.,
   P.O. Box 6651, Baulkhaun Hills, Business Centre,
   NSW 2153, Australia

ISBN 0-8069-0810-6

CONTENTS

INTRODUCTION

What is Duplicate Stitch?

Duplicate stitch embroidery, also called Swiss darning, is a technique that knitters have long used to enhance plain knitting or to add to knitted motifs. Recently, more and more people, who enjoy embroidery and needlepoint but who don't knit, have realized that they can use duplicate stitch on purchased sweaters to create beautiful surface designs. Even people who have never held a needle except to sew on a button can learn this simple technique. Duplicate stitch enables the novice and the skilled needlecrafter to transform a plain sweater into the kind made by experienced knitters or that we admire in expensive boutiques.

Duplicate is the key word to this technique. Duplicate stitch embroidery is the simple duplication of a knitted stitch to produce a motif, usually in a different color, and occasionally in a different kind of yarn. It can complement a design already knitted into a sweater or stand alone. It can add small sections of color to a larger area of color, such as adding a slightly darker shade of green to a leaf to give the impression of a shadow. Duplicate stitch embroidery can turn a plain blue sweater into an ocean with jumping dolphin, or into the sky with a flying airplane.

How the Book is Organized

This book is organized by types of motifs. In each chapter, you may find sweaters for men, women and children. Although you may not want to put a teddy bear on a man's sweater, most of the motifs can be used on a sweater for anyone. There are certain motifs that sweater designers seem to favor, such as flowers and geometric designs, and you'll find a delightful array of these kinds of patterns. In addition, you'll find beautiful and distinctive sweaters for winter and summer, sweaters that speak out with words and pictures, and sweaters that look good enough to eat.

The sweaters shown in this book were originally designed for the hand or machine knitter, but it is obvious that the motif charts also can be used on purchased sweaters which are knit to approximately the same gauge.

How to Determine Gauge

Gauge, as used throughout the book, is the number of stitches and rows in a 4-inch square. To determine gauge on a finished sweater, you can use a gauge counter, or you can mark a 4-inch square on a section of plain (Stockinette) knitting, using pins to mark the sides and corner. Lay a tape measure across the square, and with a pointed implement such as a needle or pin, count the number of stitches. Take care not to stretch the fabric as you are counting. Each stitch looks like a V on the right side of the garment. Using the pin to count stitches will help keep the stitches from "swimming" as you try to distinguish one stitch from another. Then, measure the number of rows by laying the tape measure vertically from marker to marker. Some people prefer to count rows on the wrong side of the knitting because each ridge equals one row.

Gauge is usually written as in the following example: 4" = 20 sts x 26 rows (sts is the knitting abbreviation for stitches). Figure 1 shows how to measure on a 4-inch swatch and on a 1-inch square. Measure as large an area as you can to get the most accurate measurement, and determine the gauge based on a 4-inch area.

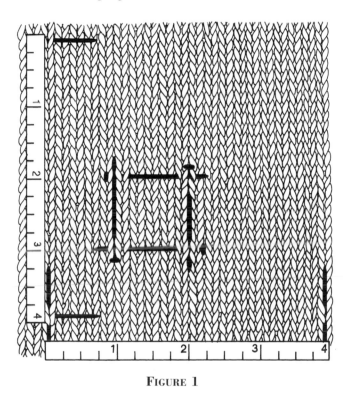

FIGURE 1

It may be difficult to measure gauge on a sweater in a store, but there is nothing wrong with taking the sweater into the dressing room and roughly measuring the gauge there. Once you determine that the gauge is close to what you are looking for, buy the sweater. If it is not worn or damaged, you can return the sweater if it does not meet your needs.

As a rule of thumb, there are usually about one-third more rows than stitches in any 4-inch square. Designers often design their motifs on "knitting graph paper," which uses rectangles instead of squares. Each grid on the knitting graph paper is ten squares wide and 14 rows high. This gives the designer a better sense of the proportion of the finished design. If you embroider a motif designed for one gauge on a significantly different gauge sweater, the design may look much bigger, smaller, or in the worst case, out of proportion from the original.

Advice For Beginners

If you have no embroidery experience, you should make your first project one with a medium or large gauge because larger stitches are easier to identify. It is also a good idea starting out to choose a light colored sweater because light colored stitches are easier to discern than dark or black stitches. Experienced needlecrafters often enlarge charts using a photocopier to make the charts easier to read.

If you want to practice duplicate stitch before you actually try the technique on a new sweater, go to a second-hand shop and purchase a sweater in the same fiber and gauge as the design you want to try in the book. Look for a "good as new," light colored sweater with clearly defined stitches. Stitches on a sweater that has been washed many times can appear to blend together, and this makes them hard to work with.

Each project in the book is designated simple, intermediate or complex. Since duplicate stitch embroidery is a very easy technique, these levels of difficulty were determined by the number of colors used and the number of stitches in the motif. We rated a small motif that requires ten or more colors as harder to work than an overall design that uses only one color. Geometric motifs or ones that repeat a design are, in general, easier to work because of the repetition of the design; the vegetable motifs in the book, for example, are rated complex because of their unique characteristics and lack of recurring elements.

When deciding which sweaters you want to attempt, be sure to factor in the gauge which we have defined as large, medium, fine and very fine. A complex pattern in a very fine gauge obviously will be more of a challenge than an intermediate design in a medium gauge. If you've never worked duplicate stitch embroidery or followed a chart, try one of the simple motifs first in a large or medium gauge. Another good strategy if you're a beginner is to consider embroidering only one aspect of a motif. For example, you can isolate one seashell from the overall design and work that over the entire sweater rather than try to complete all ten variations shown in the chart.

Fiber Content

The fiber content of the original sweater also is provided. Just because the sweater was originally knit in wool, however, doesn't mean you can't embroider your design onto a cotton or acrylic sweater. But you should be aware that a different fiber may give your finished sweater a different look from what you see in the book. The fiber content of the embroidery yarn is important, also. Unless the Key to Chart calls for embroidery floss, you should try to match the fiber content of the duplicate stitch embroidery with the yarn used in the sweater. Matching the yarn will ensure that the surface design you add will best complement the sweater.

There are two ways to use the charts in this book. The first is to find a sweater that is knit in plain Stockinette stitch and measure the gauge. Then look through the designs and choose one that fits your sweater. This is a great technique to embellish the sweaters you already own. The second way is to find a motif or design you like and buy a ready-to-wear sweater that has the required gauge or one that has the same ratio between stitches and rows. In either case, you have to be adaptable because it is unlikely you will find a sweater that has the exact gauge as the one in the book. This is where your good judgement and ability to "fudge" comes in. Here are a few examples.

Adjusting for Gauge Differences

If the motif you want to embroider is based on a gauge of 21 stitches x 28 rows gauge, then you know the ratio is three stitches to four rows. That is, three stitches take as much space horizontally as do four rows vertically. If you were embroidering a simple square, you would need three stitches and four rows. If the gauge were 24 stitches x 30 rows, the ratio would be 4:5, which means that to embroider a square you would need four stitches and five rows.

Of course, not all gauges work out to such nice even ratios. This is where the fudge factor comes in. If your gauge was 22 stitches x 26 rows, the ratio would be 11:13. If you wanted a large square, it would be easy to duplicate stitch over 11 stitches, 13 rows high, and you would have 2-inch squares. The squares using the other ratios would be much smaller, closer to a 1/2-inch square. To make a 1/2-inch square with the gauge, you would have to work over three stitches (2.76 exactly) and three or four rows (3.25 exactly). Since we rounded up the number of stitches, we would have to round up the second number. If you were to duplicate stitch using this ratio, you would probably embroider three stitches and three rows, then eyeball the square and add another row if needed.

Here is an actual example. Once I had to convert a heavy lopi style sweater to a worsted weight cotton. The gauge went from 14 stitches x 18 rows on the wool to 20 stitches x 26 rows on the cotton. When

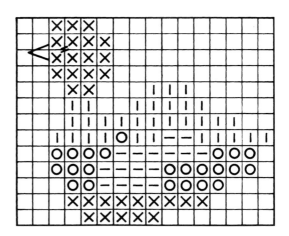

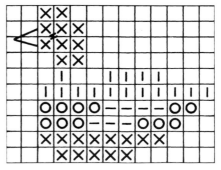

FIGURE 2

converting a duck motif chart, I knew I needed about one-third more stitches in width and height. Unfortunately, this estimate did not take into account the fact that I could not embroider over a fraction of a stitch. In order to make the ducks look proportionate, I had to fudge the chart. Then, while I embroidered, I adjusted (Figure 2). This is the tremendous advantage of duplicate stitch over knitting. Often, you can't tell until you've completed a design if it needs adjustment. If the motif is knit in, many rows have to be pulled out. If embroidered, only a few stitches need to be undone.

You also may want to use the charts in this book for other kinds of needlecraft. For instance, I once wanted a filet crochet curtain for a long window next to the front door of a house in Florida. I found a flamingo motif in a knitting book and adapted it to filet crochet. Since the crochet swatch had a gauge with a different ratio than the knitting, it was necessary to add a few rows to the body, neck and legs to achieve the same proportion as the knitted flamingo. However, the final result was perfect. Since most cross stitch and needlepoint designs are based on squares rather than rectangles, you will have to adjust. Pick a chart with as little difference as possible between stitch and row count. Remember, you can always pull out the thread and adjust.

How to Do Duplicate Stitch

Duplicate stitch embroidery is a lot like cross stitch embroidery in its technique. With basting thread, mark the area to be embroidered. Use a blunt tip, large-eyed needle, called a tapestry or yarn needle. Insert the threaded needle from the inside (wrong side) to the outside (right side) of the sweater at the base of a stitch (the base of the V-shape), and pull the needle through to the outside, leaving a tail of yarn on the inside. With the needle, trace the right side of the V (as compared to the left side), and insert the needle at the top of the right side of the V and under the base of the stitch above, reinserting the point of the needle at the top of the left leg of the V. This will put the needle on the outside of the work. Now, insert the needle at the point of entry (Figures 3, 4, 5, and 6).

Adjust the tension on the thread so as to cover the stitch below, but without pulling so tightly that you pucker the knitting underneath. Some needlecrafters assure coverage of the knitted stitches by alternating their rows in this way: On one row, they cover the knitted stitch from the right side of the V to the left side of the V; on the next row, they duplicate stitch from the left side of the V to the right side of stitch. Experiment and find the method that works best for you. Duplicate stitch sounds much more complicated than it really is. If you know a needlecrafter, ask her to show you how to do the technique. Or visit your local yarn shop and ask a salesperson to give you a 5-minute lesson. After you have worked the first few stitches, you will be an expert.

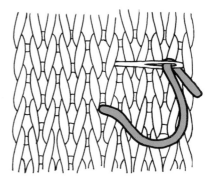

FIGURE 3

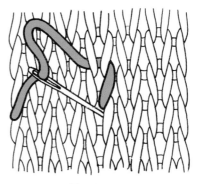

FIGURE 4

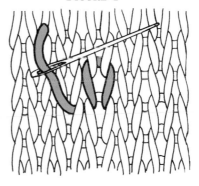

FIGURE 5

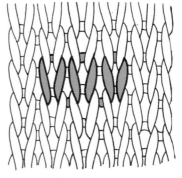

FIGURE 6

There are a few other tips that will improve the overall finished effect. If you are working many stitches of one color in a row, it is best to work across the row, then move one stitch up and work in the opposite direction across the row above. In some cases, you will work vertically rather than horizontally. Assuming that the stitches of one color are close together, it is best to work one color at a time, then go on to another color.

This approach avoids winding up with many loose tails on the inside. You can work in any direction you like as long as you frequently check the inside of the work to make sure your chosen method is neat. This is especially important on a cardigan where other people can see the inside of the sweater. Carrying strands of yarn over many stitches to get to the next section will give the wrong side of the work a messy appearance.

Most cross stitchers or needlepointers say to never make a knot on the inside, but unlike embroidery work, sweaters are meant to be worn and will therefore get stretched, and frequently be laundered. Consequently, extra care must be taken to secure the yarn ends. When a color is completed or you run out of yarn, cut a one to two-inch tail and loosely weave it through strands between stitches on the inside. You may use the yarn needle or a small crochet hook to grab the tail and twist it under and around the strands. Never begin a new strand of yarn with a knot because the knot will pull to the outside and unravel the stitches. The best technique for securing tails is to catch any long strands of previous stitches across the inside with new stitches, then weave in any remaining tails.

In some of the designs in this book, a few other types of embroidery stitches are used, primarily outline and stem stitch (Figures 7 and 8). These plain stitches are used to "draw" thin lines and are worked over knitted or duplicate stitches.

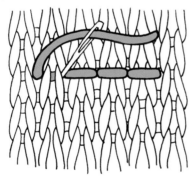

FIGURE 7

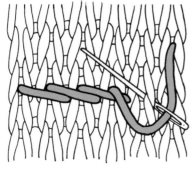

FIGURE 8

How Much Yarn You'll Need

It is hard to make a general rule about how much yarn you'll need for each color in the projects you choose. In a big motif with only a few colors, you many want to

buy a full 50-gram ball of yarn for each color. Some stores, especially those specializing in machine knitting and needlepoint, sell yarn by the ounce so that you can buy many colors inexpensively. Usually, one ounce of matching yarn is more than enough for most supplementary colors. If you can't find small quantities of matching yarn, you may want to substitute embroidery floss or tapestry wool which you can buy in small amounts in a wide range of colors.

Craft stores often sell bags of assorted colors of floss that can provide all the basic colors for very little money. Then you can buy any other colors separately. In most cases, one or two skeins of embroidery floss is all you will need per color unless many strands are used in each stitch. Make a note of the dye lot number so you can purchase more of the exact color if you need it.

Some of the patterns in this book originally called for embroidery floss. If different numbers of strands are used for different colors, the design acquires a sense of depth, with the thicker stitches more prominent than those worked with fewer strands. If no number of strands is indicated in the pattern or if you are using floss instead of the same weight yarn, you will have to experiment until you find how many strands are needed to cover the underlying stitches. Start by using the six-strand length floss as it is packaged, and adjust as needed. Often the underlying color of the sweater will partially show, especially if the stitch is pulled a little too tightly, instead of resting directly on top of the stitch. But this hint of background color can give the motif depth and can actually enhance the design.

It's important to remember that in working any of the designs in this book your goal is not to duplicate the sweater, but rather to use duplicate stitch to create your own version of the design. You can change the colors of the design, the color, style or fiber of the sweater, the placement of the motif, and make dozens of other creative choices.

For example, the vegetable sweaters originally used a knit-in checked background as the backdrop for the duplicate stitch design. You have the option of embroidering checks, finding a sweater with a similar geometric pattern, or working the motif on a solid color background. Other sweaters, such as the sailboat motifs, have more than one shade of blue knitted in to represent, in this case, the sky and the sea. Again, you can embroider the background, find a sweater with similar multi-shades of blue, or embroider the motif on a solid blue sweater (or on any color sweater you want!).

The various choices open to you are what make this approach so much fun. If you want a sweater that looks like hundreds of others, you can go to any department store and buy one. On the other hand, if you want a handmade, original design without the work of knitting the entire sweater, you can use these projects to duplicate stitch your very own creation.

PROBLEM	CAUSE	SOLUTION
Background color showing	Embroidery yarn too thin	Use more strands of floss or thicker yarn; alternate rows stitching right to left, then left to right.
	Embroidered stitches too tight	Loosen the stitches.
Puckered sweater	Embroidered stitches too tight	Loosen the stitches.
Messy inside of sweater	Unsystematic stitching	Embroider the color used the most first, working right to left on one row, then left to right on next row. Catch the strands of old stitches with new stitches.
Stitches coming undone	Ends of embroidery floss becoming unattached	Leave a tail at the beginning and end of stitching, catch tail as you stitch, complete and weave in all carefully.
Chart is too small to read	Chart *is* small so as to fit in book	Enlarge chart with a photocopier.
Stitches are hard to see	Fuzzy yarn or dark color	Choose a light-colored, smooth-finished sweater.
Design proportions are not the same as original	The ratio of stitches to rows is different on the original design	Adjust by adding or subtracting rows and stitches.

FLOWERS

BEADED BEAUTY

EARTH TONES PROVIDE A DUSKY BACKGROUND AGAINST WHICH
THE GOLD FLOWERS AND BEADS SEEM TO SHIMMER IN THE SUN.

Intermediate

Large Gauge

Original fiber used: Cotton

Gauge: 14 sts x 20 rows

Size of motif: 68 sts x 87 rows

Center chart on the upper
front of the sweater. Use three
large beads to each flower center, and use the smaller beads
on leaves as shown in chart.
Sew on beads with embroidery
yarn after you have completed
the duplicate stitch flowers.

Use one strand of same weight
yarn as sweater.

Use nine large gold-colored
beads, and 45 small gold-
colored beads.

CENTER

KEY TO CHART

⊠ = brown

▢ = ochre

• = ecru

▢ = khaki (background color)

— = outline stitch in gold

◯ = bead

FLOWER LATTICE

PINK ROSES AND A LATTICE LEND AN OLD FASHIONED
AND FEMININE QUALITY TO THIS CHARMING CARDIGAN.

Intermediate

Fine Gauge

Original fiber used: Wool

Gauge: 23 sts x 31 rows

Size of motif: 70 sts x 88 rows

Center chart on each front panel of the cardigan.
The flower motifs may be embroidered with or
without the connecting lattice.

Use indicated number of strands of tapestry wool
for the embroidery.

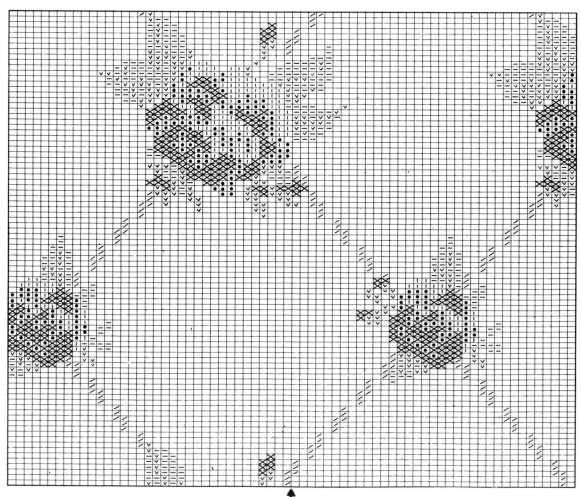

CENTER

TULIPS

PRETTY ENOUGH TO PICK, THE TULIPS ON THIS CHEERFUL
SWEATER WILL STAY FRESH ALL YEAR LONG.

Intermediate

Medium Gauge

Original fiber used: Cotton

Gauge: 19 sts x 26 rows

Size of each tulip motif: 20 sts x 63 rows

Embroider four tulips on the front, three tulips on
the back, and three tulips on each sleeve. You can
create a different look by choosing a sweater with
another background color.

Use one strand of same weight yarn as sweater.

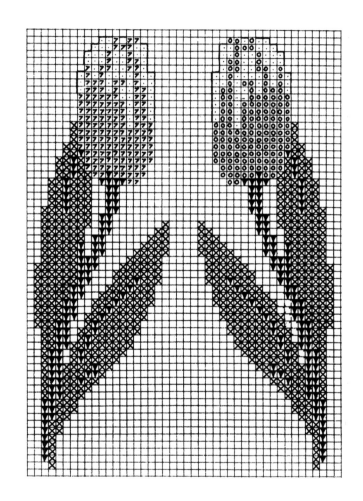

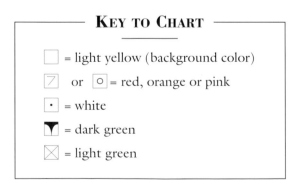

KEY TO CHART

☐ = light yellow (background color)

⬗ or ⊙ = red, orange or pink

· = white

▼ = dark green

⊠ = light green

WILDFLOWER

CAPTURE THE BEAUTY OF WILDFLOWERS AND
HERBS IN THIS LOVELY GARDEN DESIGN.

Complex

Fine Gauge

Original fiber used: Cotton

Gauge: 24 sts x 32 rows

Size of largest motif: 24 sts x 46 rows

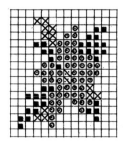
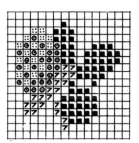

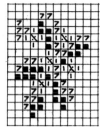
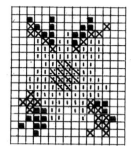

Counting stitches and rows, divide front and back of sweater into nine equal sections, and sleeves into four large sections plus two half sections at the top of sleeve, using basting thread to mark off boxes. Duplicate stitch each large motif in each large section and two small motifs at the top of each sleeve. Embroider in cross stitch, duplicate stitch or outline stitch as desired between squares. If you prefer, you can choose to embroider any of these motifs individually.

Use one strand of same weight yarn as sweater.

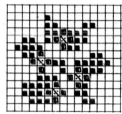

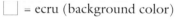

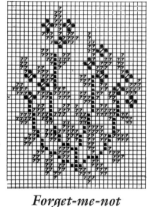

Forget-me-not

Plantain

Basil

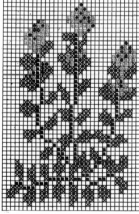

Thyme

Mint

Sage

KEY TO CHARTS

- ☐ = ecru (background color)
- ■ = green
- ☒ = gray green
- ⊙ = pink
- ⊡ = light yellow
- ⠿ = light pink
- ◸ = bright green
- ⊟ = white
- ◧ = turquoise
- ⊻ = brown
- ⊞ = khaki
- ◿ = yellow
- ⫿ = lilac
- ◤ = gold

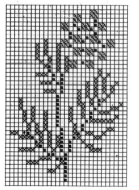

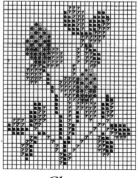

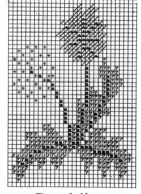

Goldenrod

Clover

Dandelion

SPRING FLOWERS

AS IF SCATTERED BY A SOFT BREEZE, SPRING FLOWERS
FLUTTER ACROSS THIS LOVELY CARDIGAN.

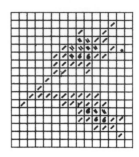

Intermediate

Fine Gauge

Original fiber used: Cotton

Gauge: 24 sts x 36 rows

Size of largest motif: 53 sts x 49 rows

Scatter the motifs wherever you like and make
as many as you like to decorate the front, back
and sleeves.

Use one length of six-strand embroidery floss
for each color.

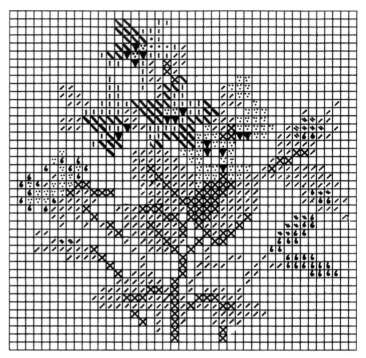

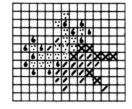

KEY TO CHARTS

☐ = pink (background color)

◩ = light green

☒ = green

◺ = dark pink

❟ = red

⁙ = yellow

◣ = blue

◫ = light blue

▼ = brown

∙ = ecru

LEAVES

Intermediate

Large Gauge

Original fiber used: Wool

Gauge: 15 sts x 20 rows

Size of motif: 95 sts x 136 rows

THIS LOVELY SWEATER PAYS TRIBUTE TO THE SIMPLE YET
BEAUTIFUL PATTERNS FOUND IN THE HUMBLE LEAF.

Center chart on the front and sleeves. You can
choose to embroider just one leaf motif or you
can use them all. Any combination of colors will
result in an attractive sweater.

Use one strand of same weight yarn as sweater,
or 12 strands of tapestry wool.

KEY TO CHART

☐ = background color

● = green

○ = bright green

⊠ = dark blue

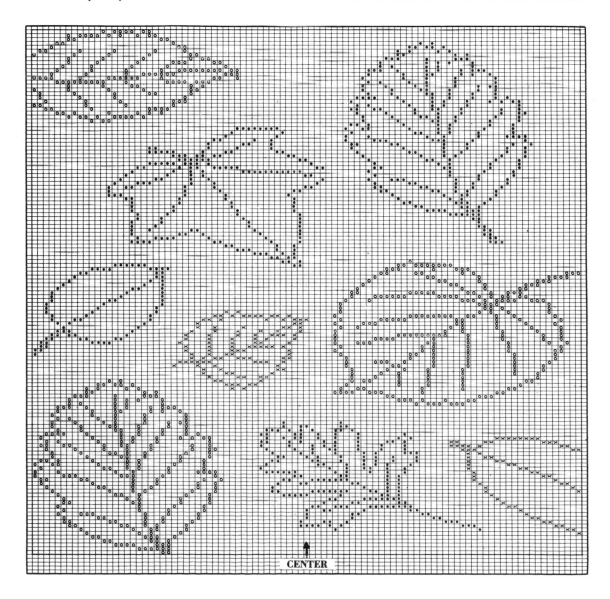

CENTER

POPPIES

BRIGHT, RED POPPIES ARE THE FOCAL POINT OF THE
FLOWER BOUQUETS IN THIS PRETTY, SUMMERY SWEATER.

KEY TO CHART

☐ = background color
☒ = moss green
◩ = grass green
◪ = medium green
◺ = light green
● = dark blue
⊟ = medium blue
⊟ = red
◲ = gray
⧄ = dark yellow
◫ = light yellow
◹ = white
◧ = black

Intermediate

Fine Gauge

Original fiber used: Cotton

Gauge: 21 sts x 25 rows

Size of motif: 65 sts x 72 rows

On the front of the sweater, embroider one bouquet upper right and one bouquet lower left, and one bouquet on each sleeve. A plain background will make the floral motifs even more dramatic.

Use three strands of black embroidery floss, and seven strands embroidery floss for all other colors.

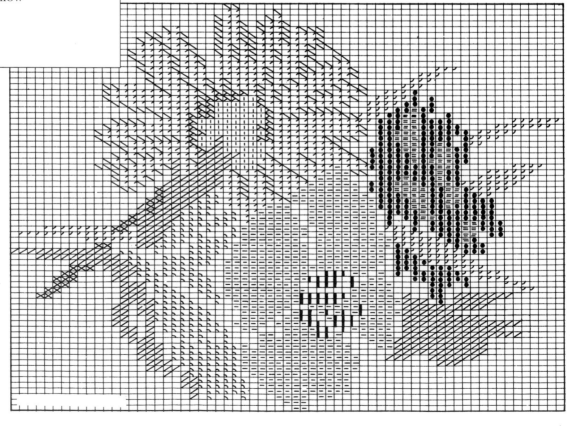

BLOOMING ROSES

THE COLORFUL ROSES ON THIS PULLOVER ARE SURE
TO BRING OUT THE SMILE ON ANY BABY'S FACE.

Intermediate

Very Fine Gauge

Original fiber used: Cotton

Gauge: 26 sts x 38 rows

Size of large motif: 78 sts x 86 rows

Size of small motif: 63 sts x 58 rows

Center the large motif on the front and center the
small motif on the sleeves.

Use one strand of same weight yarn as sweater.

KEY TO CHART

SMALL MOTIF

☐ = turquoise

▯ = green

⊞ = dark green

⊟ = yellow

⊠ = orange

▱ = pink

● = dark pink

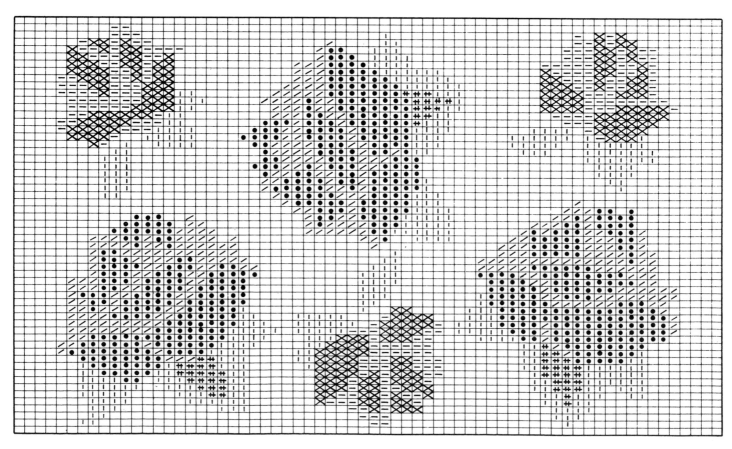

(Large motif continued on page 28)

BLOOMING ROSES

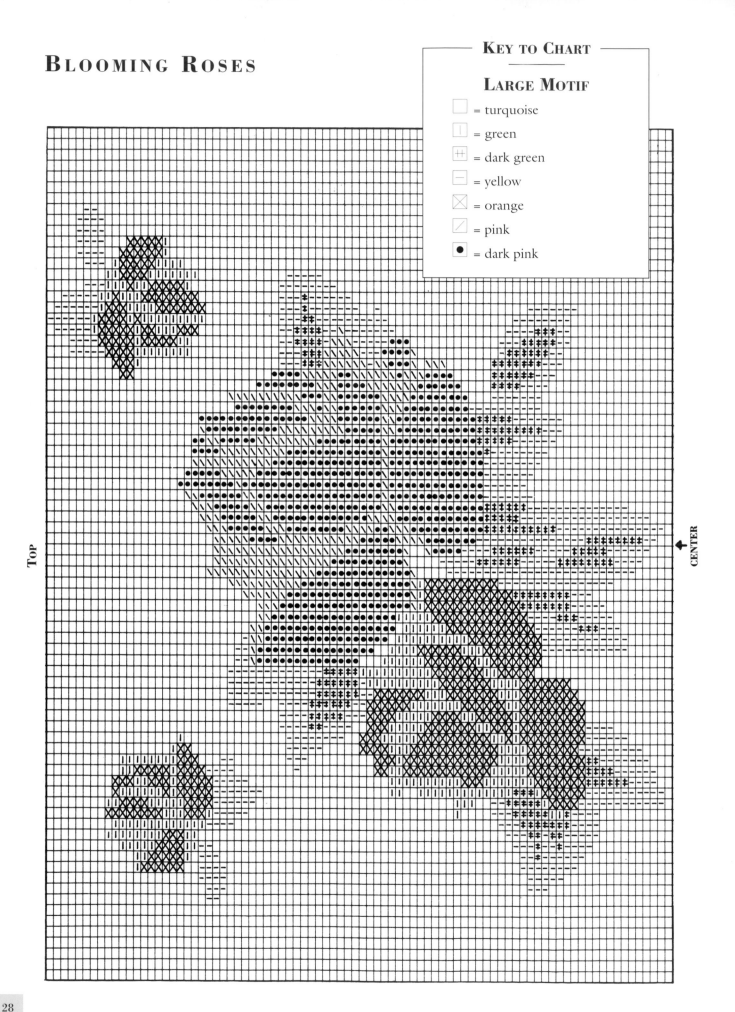

KEY TO CHART

LARGE MOTIF

☐ = turquoise
⊡ = green
⊞ = dark green
⊟ = yellow
⊠ = orange
◹ = pink
● = dark pink

TOP

CENTER

PRETTY IN PINK

PRETTY IN PINK DESCRIBES THIS GIRL'S SWEET SWEATER,
WITH ITS SIMPLE FLOWER MOTIF.

Simple

Medium Gauge

Original fiber used: Wool

Gauge: 19 sts x 26 rows

Size of motif: 6 sts x 15 rows

Stagger the motifs across the front of the sweater, spaced 10 stitches and four rows apart. The flowers also can be scattered randomly.

Use one strand of same weight yarn as sweater.

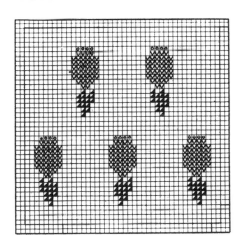

KEY TO CHART

☐ = pink (background color)

◢ = green

⊙ = light pink

▽ = dark pink

DIAMONDS AND FLOWERS

DIAMONDS IN COMPLEMENTARY HUES PROVIDE DISTINCTIVE FRAMES FOR
SHOWCASING EACH PERFECT JEWEL OF A ROSE.

Intermediate

Fine Gauge

Original fiber used: Wool

Gauge: 24 sts x 33 rows

Size of motif: 38 sts x 76 rows

Repeat the flower motif across the front of the
sweater. Frame the motif in diamonds or let them
stand alone. The original sweater has a row of
diamonds at the bottom. If you feel ambitious,
you can duplicate stitch these, too, by repeating
the diamond motif without the flower inside.

Use one strand of same weight yarn as sweater
or four strands of tapestry wool.

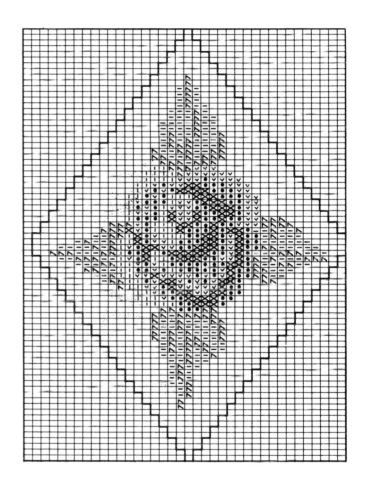

KEY TO CHART

☐ = background color for
diamonds (should contrast
with color of sweater)

⊟ = light green

◺ = olive green

⊠ = rose

⬤ = pink

V = medium pink

⫼ = light pink

31

CENTER

Country Day

Gentle colors and garden-fresh patterns evoke a romantic day in the country.

Complex

Very Fine Gauge

Original fiber used: Linen

Gauge: 26 sts x 35 rows

Size of motif: 168 sts x 234 rows

Center chart on the back, front and sleeves of the sweater. There is a tremendous difference in the number of strands used, and this gives depth to the flowers.

Used indicated number of strands of embroidery floss.

Key to Chart

- ☐ = pink (background color)
- ⊡ = white - 4 strands
- ⊟ = green - 14 strands
- | = light green - 13 strands
- ⧄ = light yellow - 4 strands
- ⊞ = yellow - 4 strands
- ⁘ = bright yellow - 1 strand
- L = light blue - 1 strand
- ⊠ = burgandy - 7 strands
-) = light salmon - 3 strands
- 1⁄ = lilac - 3 strands
- ⧅ = light brick red - 5 strands
- ☰ = brick red - 5 strands
- (= light lilac - 2 strands
- ∝ = blue - 1 strand

CLIMBING GARDEN

PINK FLOWERS PROUDLY BLOOM ON THIS DAZZLING
PULLOVER, CAPTURING THE SPIRIT OF SPRINGTIME.

Complex

Fine Gauge

Original fiber used: Cotton

Gauge: 22 sts x 30 rows

Size of motif: 134 sts x 167 rows

Center chart on the front of the sweater. The
unembroidered sleeves and back focus attention
on the detailed front motif.

Use one strand of same weight yarn as sweater.

KEY TO CHART

☐ = ecru (background color)

● = blue gray

— = gray

| = old rose

☒ = light green

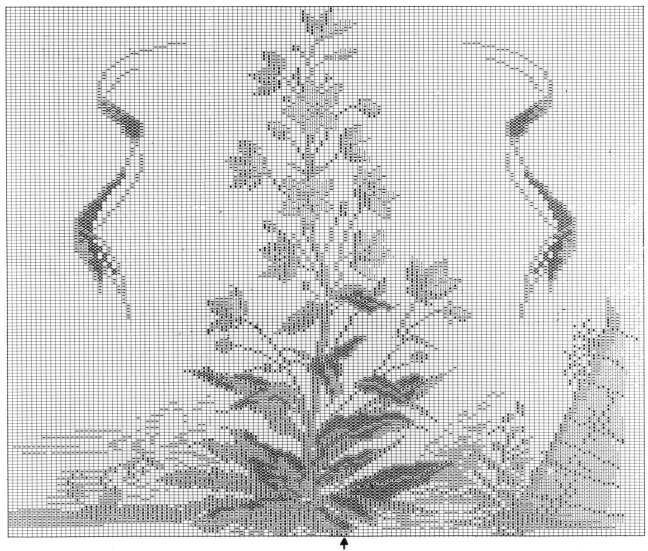

↑
CENTER

GEOMETRIC PATTERNS

A R A B I A N   D A Y S

SIMPLE ARABIC LINES ON A DESERT-NEUTRAL BACKGROUND
CREATE A DRAMATIC AND TIMELESS SWEATER.

Intermediate

Large Gauge

Original fiber used: Wool

Gauge: 17 sts x 21 rows

Size of motif: 114 sts x 138 rows

Center chart on the back, front and sleeves of
the sweater.

Use one strand of same weight yarn as sweater.

KEY TO CHART

- ● = black
- ☐ = beige
  (background color)

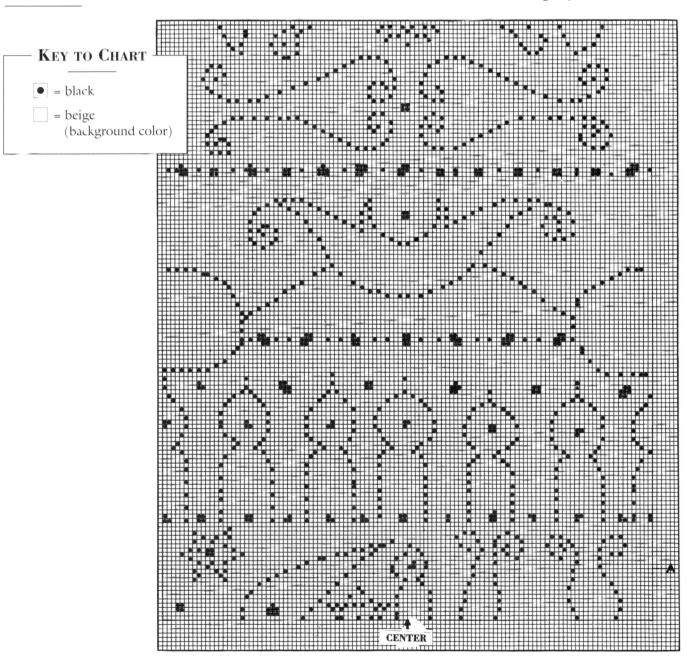

CENTER

A

JAZZY JACQUARD

INTRICATE PATTERNS AND BOLD COLORS COMBINE
TO CREATE A TOTALLY STUNNING SWEATER.

Complex

Medium Gauge

Original fiber used: Cotton

Gauge: 19 sts x 22 rows

Size of motif: 33 sts x 59 rows

Center the chart on the back, front, and sleeves of
the sweater. The chart can be repeated for an all-
over design or only once along the lower edge.

Use one strand of same weight yarn as sweater.

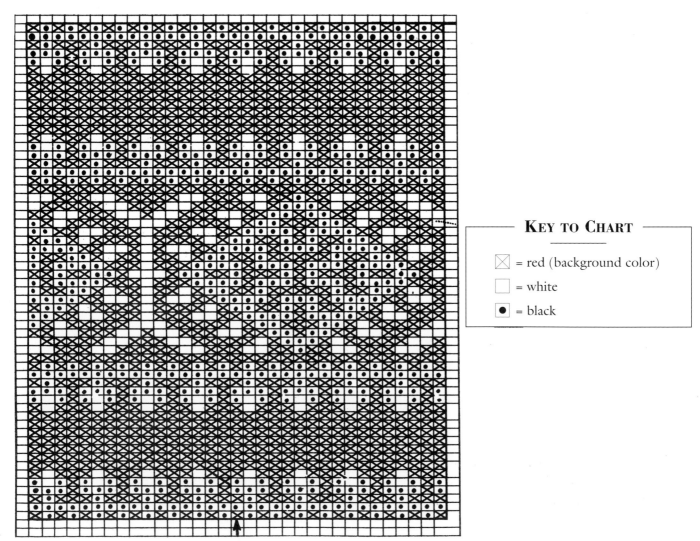

CENTER

KEY TO CHART

⊠ = red (background color)

☐ = white

⊙ = black

RED BANDANNA

THE FAMILIAR MOTIF ON THIS GORGEOUS SWEATER ELEVATES
THE HUMBLE RED BANDANNA TO NEW HEIGHTS OF FASHION.

Complex

Very Fine Gauge

Original fiber used: Cotton

Gauge: 27 sts x 33 rows

Size of motif: 152 sts x 158 rows

Center chart on back and front of sweater. Center
dark blue band on lower edge of each sleeve. Be
sure you can embroider the entire motif on the
front so the edges can be seen completely.

Use one strand of same weight yarn as sweater.

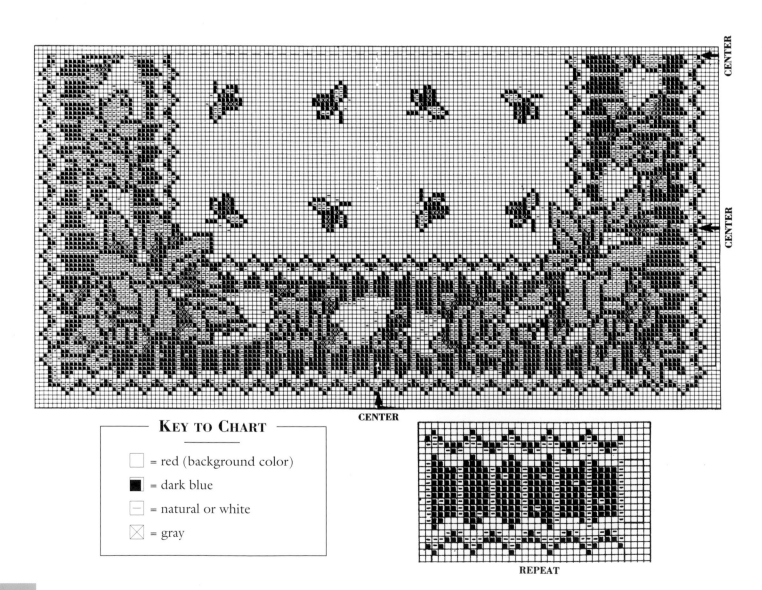

KEY TO CHART

☐ = red (background color)

■ = dark blue

⊟ = natural or white

☒ = gray

REPEAT

POLKA DOTS

BUNDLE THE BABY IN SUNSHINE
WITH THIS YELLOW POLKA DOT MOTIF.

Simple

Very Fine Gauge

Original fiber used: Cotton

Gauge: 26 sts x 36 rows

Size of motif: 8 sts x 10 rows

Scatter the polka dots on the front, back and
sleeves of sweater. Big dots can be embroidered in
any color or combination of colors for a fun effect.

Use one strand of same weight yarn as sweater.

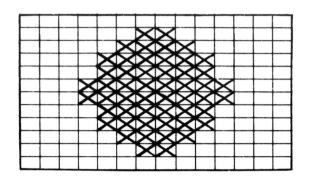

KEY TO CHART

☒ = yellow

☐ = white (background color)

BOLD STROKES

STROKE OF GENIUS APTLY DESCRIBES THE REPEATING
PATTERN ON THIS MAN'S STYLISH SWEATER.

Simple

Medium Gauge

Original fiber used: Cotton

Gauge: 19 sts x 28 rows

Size of motif: 60 sts x 47 rows

Use chart as a guide to evenly cover the sweater
with diagonal lines.

Use one strand of same weight yarn as sweater.

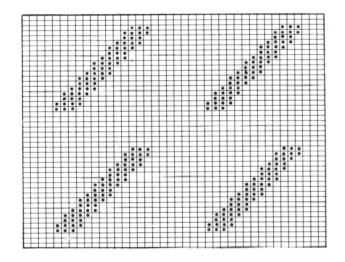

ARGYLE TWOSOME

HERE ARE TWO STRIKING REASONS WHY ARGYLE CONTINUES
TO BE SUCH A POPULAR DESIGN FOR MEN AND WOMEN.

WOMAN'S PULLOVER

Complex

Fine Gauge

Original fiber used: Wool

Gauge: 21 sts x 27 rows

Size of motif: 60 sts x 40 rows

Center chart on the back and front of the sweater.
An all-over embroidery would take a long time,
but the motif can be worked over the front only.

Use one strand of same weight yarn as sweater.

MAN'S VEST

Complex

Fine Gauge

Original fiber used: Wool

Gauge: 21 sts x 27 rows

Size of motif: 44 sts x 34 rows

Use one strand of same weight yarn as sweater.

KEY TO CHART

⊠ = dark blue (background color)

● = lavender blue

☐ = beige

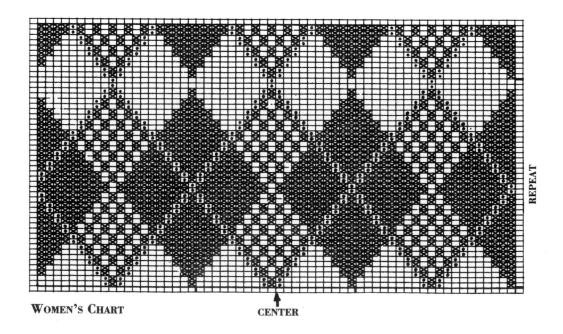

WOMEN'S CHART

CENTER

REPEAT

KEY TO CHART

□ = beige (background color)

⊠ = brown

⊡ = red

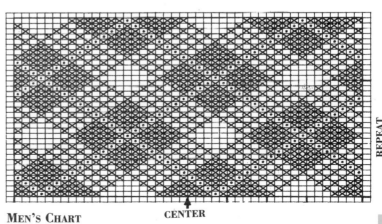

MEN'S CHART   CENTER   REPEAT

FLOWER CHART

DELFT CLASSIC

THE BOLD LINES ON THIS MAN'S SWEATER ARE REMINISCENT
OF THE CLASSIC DUTCH BLUE AND WHITE DELFT MOTIF.

Intermediate

Medium Gauge

Original fiber used: Cotton

Gauge: 19 sts x 26 rows

Size of flower motif: 116 sts x 29 rows

Size of lattice motif: 68 sts x 93 rows

Work flower chart across the sweater's lower edge,
leave two rows unembroidered, work six rows of

white duplicate stitch across all stitches, leave two
rows unembroidered, then work lattice chart over
93 rows, leave two rows unembroidered, work six
rows of white duplicate stitch across all stitches,
and leave two rows unembroidered. Alternately
embroider over four stitches in white, then leave
four stitches unembroidered across the top of
sweater. Center lattice chart over sleeve.

Use one strand of same weight yarn as sweater.

LATTICE CHART

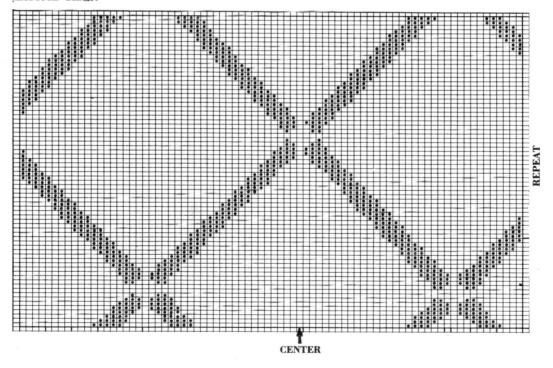

CENTER

REPEAT

KEY TO CHARTS

● = white

☐ = blue (background color)

BLOCKS OF COLOR

TWO-TONE COLOR BLOCKS STACK UP HANDSOMELY
ON THIS MAN'S SUMMER PULLOVER.

Simple

Medium Gauge

Original fiber used: Cotton

Gauge: 19 sts x 26 rows

Size of motif: 16 sts x 22 rows and 16 sts x 24 rows

Alternate bands of Chart 1 and Chart 2. If you're lucky, you'll be able to find a sweater with a stripe like the one shown in the photograph. An attractive design also can be made by using a solid sweater of a contrasting color and scattering the two blocks, using two different colors.

Use one strand of same weight yarn as sweater.

KEY TO CHARTS

☐ = blue-white tweed

☐ = white-blue tweed

CHART 1

CHART 2

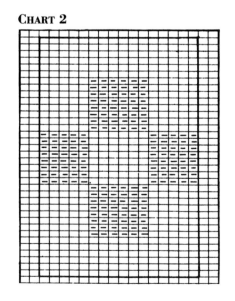

WORDS, LETTERS, AND PICTURES

HAPPY BIRTHDAY

THE CHILDLIKE LETTERING ON THIS PRECIOUS SWEATER
MAKES IT A PERFECT FIT FOR A BIRTHDAY BOY OR GIRL.

Intermediate

Very Fine Gauge

Original fiber used: Cotton

Gauge: 26 sts x 36 rows

Size of motif: 76 sts x 103 rows

Center chart on the front of the sweater. All the letters can be embroidered in the same color or in different colors as shown.

Use one strand of same weight yarn as sweater.

KEY TO CHART

1 = lavender

2 = purple

3 = violet

4 = gray green

5 = green

6 = bright green

7 = French blue

8 = dark blue

9 = yellow

10 = ochre

11 = red

12 = raspberry

SAMPLER

THIS LOVELY ALPHABET SWEATER CAN BE PERSONALIZED
FOR YOU, COUSIN SUE, OR AUNT EMMY LOU.

Complex

Fine Gauge

Original fiber used: Cotton

Gauge: 24 sts x 32 rows

Size of large motif: 140 sts x 170 rows

Center the large chart on the back and front of the sweater. Typical historical samplers show the name of the original needleworker and the date the piece was completed. You may want to stitch on your own name, the date you decorated your sweater, or you can eliminate these elements.

Use one strand of same weight yarn as sweater.

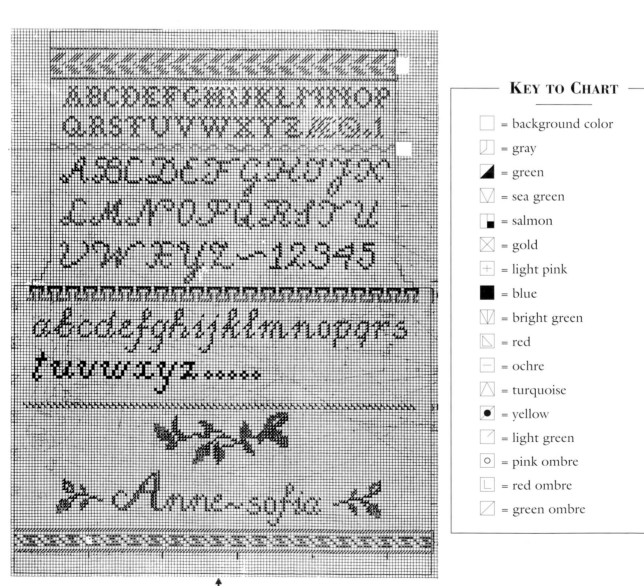

CENTER

KEY TO CHART

☐	= background color
◿	= gray
◣	= green
▽	= sea green
◳	= salmon
⊠	= gold
⊞	= light pink
■	= blue
�▽	= bright green
◹	= red
⊟	= ochre
◹	= turquoise
⦿	= yellow
◸	= light green
⊙	= pink ombre
⊔	= red ombre
◺	= green ombre

PICTURE PERFECT

THIS WHIMSICAL PULLOVER TRANSFORMS A CHILD'S
SIMPLE DRAWING INTO AN EYE-CATCHING DESIGN.

Intermediate

Medium Gauge

Original fiber used: Cotton

Gauge: 19 sts x 25 rows

Size of motif: 76 sts x 91 rows

Center chart on front. Child's drawing is adapted
to duplicate stitch. Cut four-inch strands of yarn,
and duplicate stitch diagonal lines on sleeves and
back, using photograph as a guide. Size of line is
based on length of yarn.

Use one strand of same weight yarn as sweater.

CENTER

KEY TO CHART

☐ = background color

○ = light pink

● = red

· = yellow

⊠ = green

◹ = turquoise

⊡ = purple

SWEET ROSES

THE COMBINATION OF WORDS AND FLOWERS ADDS UP TO A SPECIAL PICTURE-POEM FOR A VERY SPECIAL GIRL.

Intermediate

Very Fine

Original fiber used: Cotton

Gauge: 28 sts x 39 rows

Size of motif: 96 sts x 130 rows

Center chart on the back or front of the sweater. The floral motif can be embroidered with or without the words.

The original used embroidery floss to embroider motifs. The different number of strands of floss gives depth to the motif. Be sure to used indicated number of strands.

KEY TO CHART

- ☐ = background color
- · = white - 1 strand
- ▼ = red - 2 strands
- Z = green - 2 strands
- − = light green - 3 strands
- ● = dark green - 2 strands
- ⌒ = light dusty rose - 2 strands
- ☒ = burgundy - 1 strand
- ~ = dusty rose - 2 strands

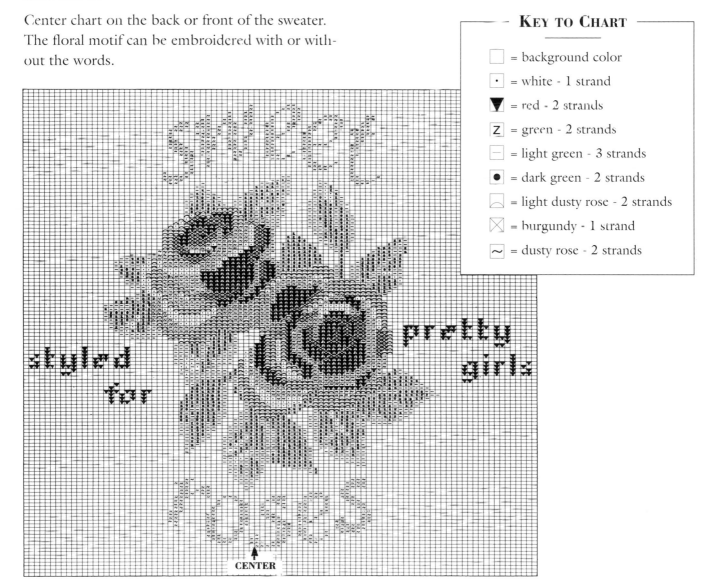

CENTER

FLIGHT OF FANCY

WITH A COLORFUL AIRPLANE SOARING THROUGH CLEAR
BLUE SKIES, THIS SWEATER CAN'T HELP TAKING OFF.

Difficult

Medium Gauge

Original fiber used: Cotton

Gauge: 20 sts x 28 rows

Size of airplane motif: 78 sts x 91 rows

Size of sleeve motif: 55 sts x 41 rows

Center airplane chart on front. Center sleeve chart
on each sleeve. Airplane motif is worked best on a
blue sweater, and looks especially good if there is
more than one shade of blue to symbolize the sky.
Optional: Embroider the word Pilot on the left
sleeve and the word Flight on the right sleeve.

Use one strand of same weight yarn as sweater.

SLEEVE MOTIF

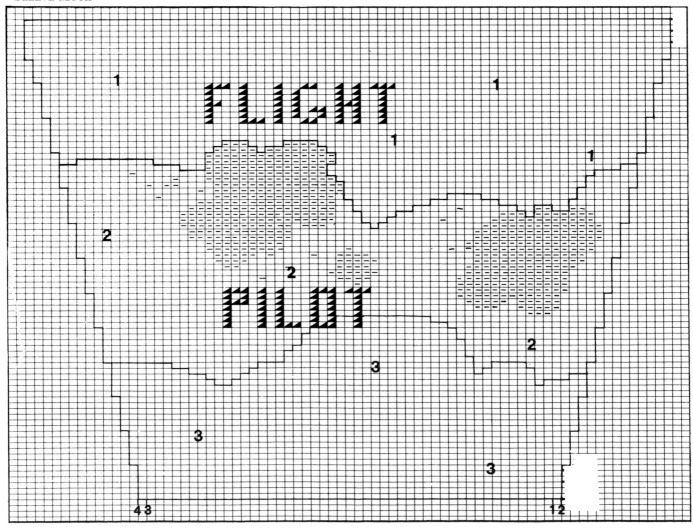

(Airplane motif continued on page 60)

FLIGHT OF FANCY

AIRPLANE MOTIF

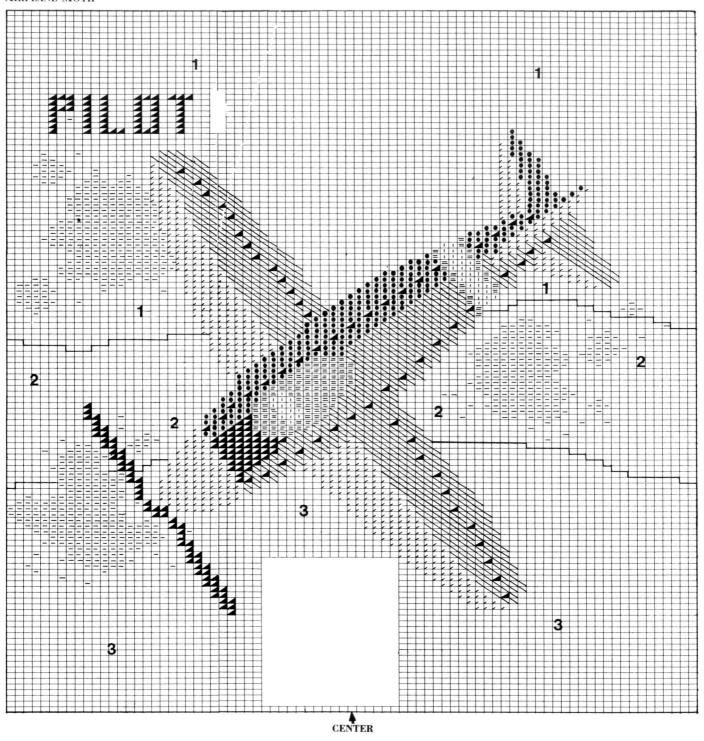

CENTER

KEY TO CHARTS

☐ = background color	🔲 = orange	⬤ = dark gray
1 = light blue	─ = white	◤ = black
☰ and 2 = dark blue	╱ = red	
3 = medium blue	�%⃥ = light gray	

CHINESE SYMBOL

CHINESE LETTERS, DRAWN IN BLACK ON A RED SWEATER,
TURN A SIMPLE DESIGN INTO A DRAMATIC STATEMENT.

Simple

Medium Gauge

Original fiber used: Wool

Gauge: 16 sts x 22 rows

Size of motif: 41 sts x 38 rows

Center chart on the front of the sweater.

Use one strand of same weight yarn as sweater.

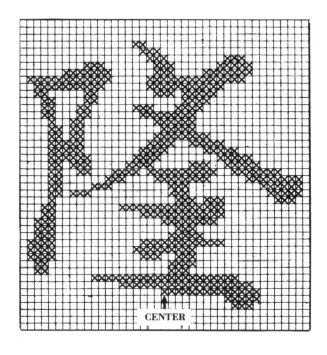

CENTER

KEY TO CHART

⊠ = black

☐ = red

TOPIARY SAMPLER

A SAMPLER AND FORMAL GARDEN MOTIF IN PRETTY PASTELS MAKE A CLASSIC CHILD'S PULLOVER.

Complex

Very Fine Gauge

Original fiber used: Cotton

Gauge: 32 sts x 45 rows

Size of motif: 130 sts x 145 rows

Center complete chart on front. Center one heart and two flowers on each sleeve, and use the snowflake-like design above wrist. Wrap letter "a" through letter "d" on chart on right sleeve above heart and flower motif, and wrap letter "f" through letter "j" on chart on left sleeve.

The original used embroidery floss to embroider motifs. Be sure to use indicated number of strands.

KEY TO CHART

- ☐ = background color
- V = beige - 1 strand
- ⊠ = dark pink - 1 strand
- · = light pink - 1 strand
- ● = blue - 1 strand
- ◿ = brown - 1 strand
- ◺ = ochre - 1 strand
- ◹ = light ochre - 1 strand
- Z = dark green - 2 strands
- — = light green - 1 strand

CENTER

BALLERINA

HERE'S A PERFECTLY DELIGHTFUL MOTIF
FOR THE LITTLE BALLERINA IN YOUR LIFE.

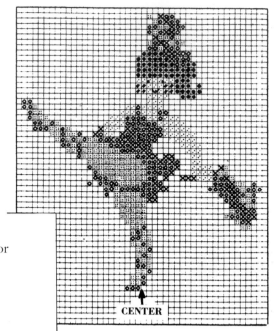

Intermediate

Very Fine Gauge

Original fiber used: Cotton

Gauge: 26 sts x 34 rows

Size of motif: 44 sts x 51 rows

Center chart on front. The original
motif is worked in cross stitch but can
be adapted easily to duplicate stitch.

Use one strand of same weight yarn as
sweater.

KEY TO CHART

☐ = background color

● = brown

∴ = white

⊘ = pink

⊠ = dark blue

○ = blue

∷ = light blue

CENTER

FRUIT SALAD

LIFE-SIZED FRUIT ON AN OVERSIZED RAGLAN SWEATER
CREATE A UNIQUE AND APPEALING DESIGN.

(Photo on preceeding page)

Intermediate

Fine Gauge

Original fiber used: Cotton

Gauge: 23 sts x 33 rows

Size of largest motif: 33 sts x 64 rows

Choose whichever fruit motifs you desire
and scatter them on the sweater. The original pattern outlines each motif in ecru, but
the motif can be worked without the outlines.

Use one strand of same weight yarn as
sweater.

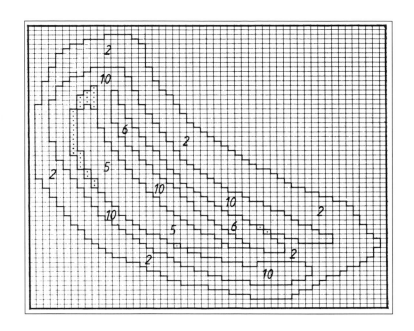

KEY TO CHART

1 = red orange

2 = ecru (motif background)

3 = orange

4 = lemon

5 = yellow

6 = ochre

7 = purple

8 = green

9 = light green

10 = black

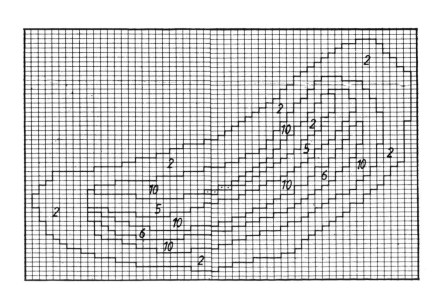

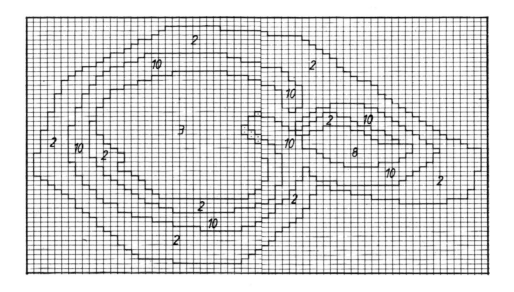

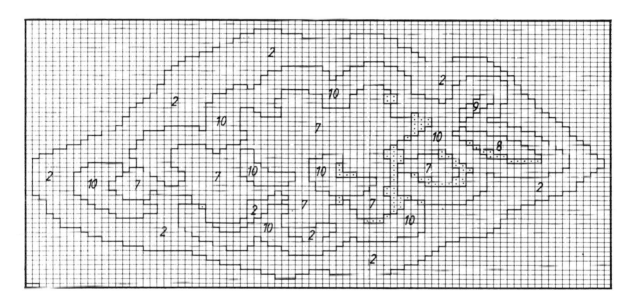

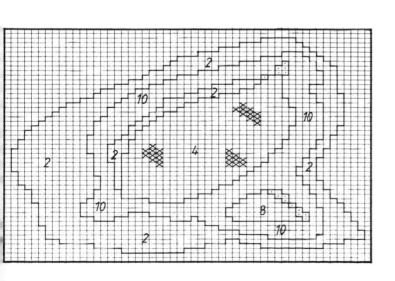

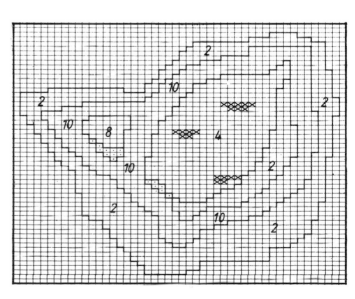

GRAPES

A BUNCH OF RICHLY COLORED GRAPES MAKES A MOUTH-WATERING DESIGN ON THIS BULKY KNIT SWEATER.

Intermediate

Large Gauge

Original fiber used: Wool

Gauge: 13 sts x 17.5 rows

Size of motif: 63 sts x 60 rows

Center chart on the back or front of the sweater. The motif will be very large on a bulky knit. If worked on a finer gauge sweater, the motif will look much smaller.

Use one strand of same weight yarn as sweater.

KEY TO CHART

☐ = background color

· = pink

·· = lilac

⬚ = light green

▼ = dark green

◪ = green

◣ = dark brown

○ = brown

⊠ = purple

● = dark red

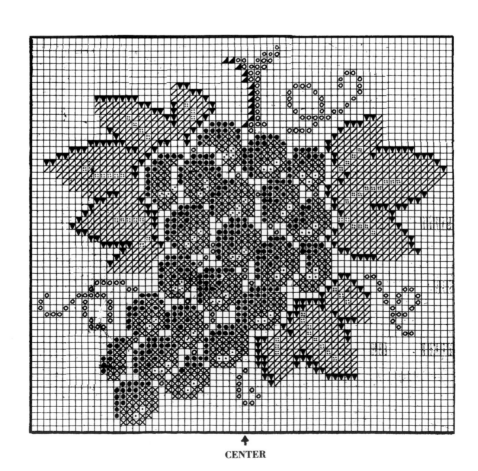

↑
CENTER

FABULOUS FRUIT DUO

VARIED SHADES OF COLOR AND INTRICATE DETAIL GIVE THESE
MOTHER AND CHILD SWEATERS THE TIMELESS LOOK OF TAPESTRY.

Complex

Medium Gauge

Original fiber used: Wool

Gauge: 19 sts x 27 rows

Size of woman's fruit motif: 106 x 85 rows

Size of child's fruit motif: 65 sts x 65 rows

Size of woman's Fair Isle motif: 16 sts x 76 rows

Size of child's Fair Isle motif: 16 sts x 76 rows

Center the large motif on the front and center the Fair Isle motif on the sleeves. If you prefer, you can embroider only the fruit motif, using the smaller fruit motifs at the lower and upper edges of the sleeves.

Use two strands of tapestry wool of same weight as sweater.

(Woman's charts are on pages 72 and 73.)

KEY TO CHART

CHILD'S FRUIT MOTIF

- ⊠ = light green
- ▼ = yellow green
- ◗ = green
- ◢ = purple
- C = lilac
- ▲ = dark red
- ⦿ = red
- ● = orange red
- V = rose red
- ○ = light rose red
- ⦿ = gray green
- ╱ = light gray green
- ╲ = dark gray green
- ⊡ = orange yellow
- ‖ = light yellow
- ═ = salmon
- ⊥ = pink
- ╱ = brown
- · = white

CENTER

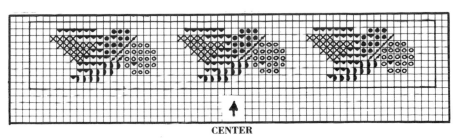

CENTER

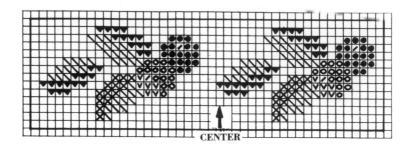

KEY TO CHART

WOMAN'S FRUIT MOTIF

- ∴ = light pink
- = = light rose
- V = rose
- ○ = pink
- ◉ = dark pink
- ● = red
- ▲ = dark red
- ◗ = dark green
- ▼ = green
- ⊠ = yellow green
- ◉ = gray green
- ◺ = light green
- ◹ = light gray green
- ◢ = purple
- C = lilac
- ╱ = brown
- ⊓ = light yellow
- ⬚ = yellow
- ⊥ = pink
- · = white

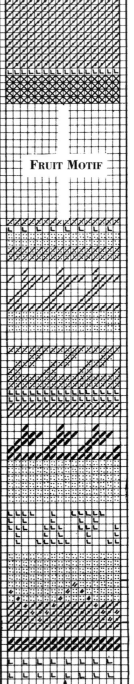

FRUIT MOTIF

FRUIT MOTIF

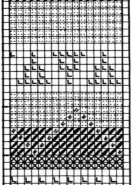

KEY TO CHARTS

FAIR ISLE MOTIF

- ⌴ = red
- ☐ = white
- ⋮ = light blue
- ⬕ = grey blue
- ╱ = dark grey blue
- ● = teal blue
- ⊠ = midnight blue
- ⬩ = rose

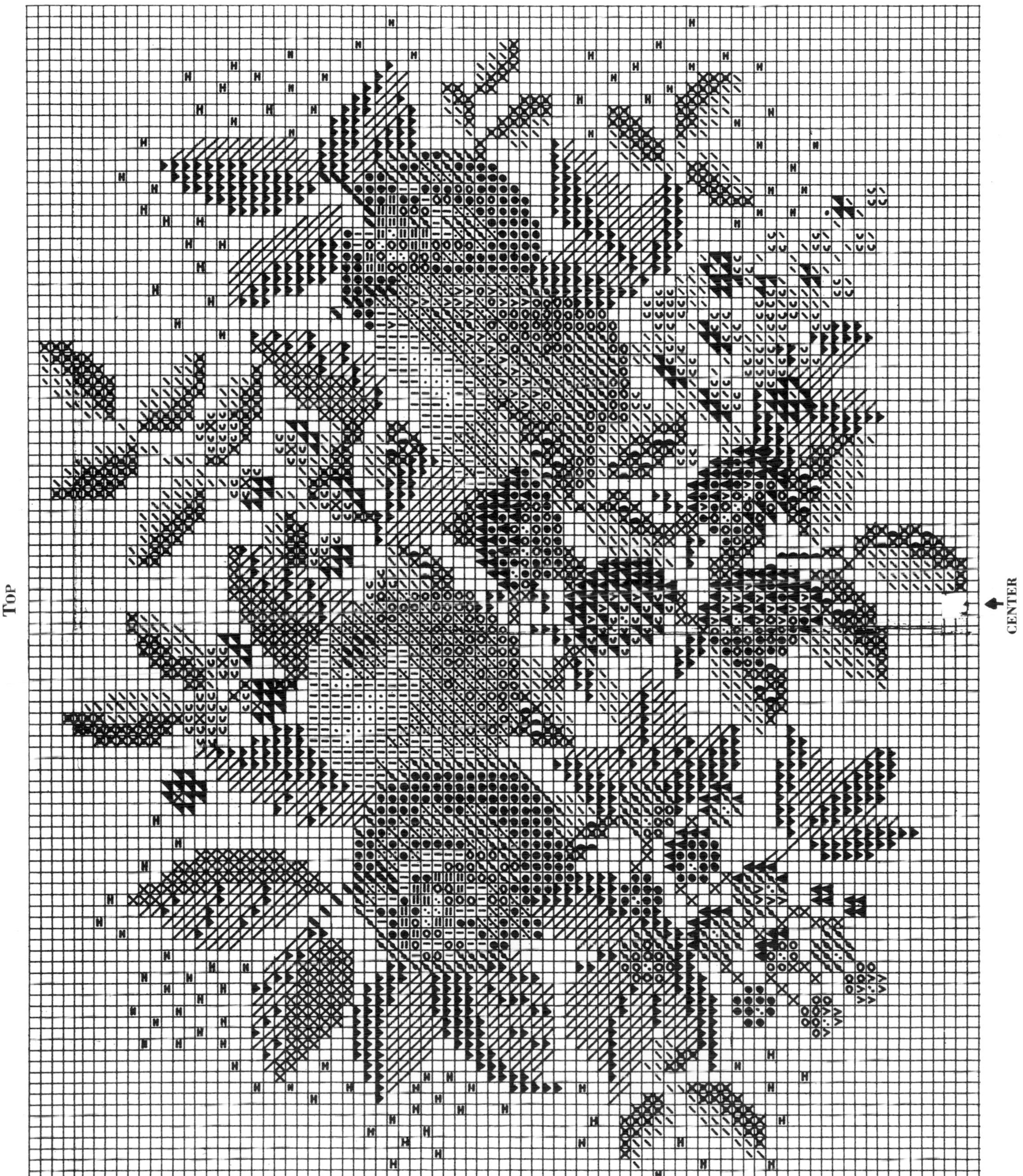
Top
Center

VEGETABLE MEDLEY I

A MARVELOUS MEDLEY OF MUSHROOMS, LEEKS, RADISHES,
AND TOMATOES MAKES A BOLD AND ATTRACTIVE DESIGN.

Complex

Medium Gauge

Original fiber used: Cotton

Gauge: 20 sts x 24 rows

Size of motif: 81 sts x 85 rows

Center chart on the front of the sweater. You may
eliminate the green checked background and use
this design on a solid color sweater that contrasts
nicely with the colors of the vegetables.

Use two strands of same weight yarn as sweater, or
an equivalent amount of embroidery floss.

(Chart is on page 78.)

KEY TO CHART

⋅	= light sea green
⊢	= dark sea green
=	= dark gray green
⊓	= blue green
▼	= bright green
⊘	= green
⋮⋮	= gray green
☐	= white
⊠	= ecru
◹	= beige
╱	= sand
∴	= khaki
■	= dark gray brown
Z	= dark orange
◺	= light orange
○	= light red
╱	= red
◣	= eggplant
▼	= dark red
U	= pink
ꝛ	= rose
⌊	= yellow

VEGETABLE MEDLEY II

THESE TRUE-TO-LIFE VEGETABLES PROVIDE ALL THE
INGREDIENTS NEEDED TO COOK UP A DELIGHTFUL SWEATER.

Complex

Medium Gauge

Original fiber used: Cotton

Gauge: 20 sts x 24 rows

Size of motif: 85 sts x 84 rows

Center chart on the back or front of the sweater.
You may eliminate the beige checked background
and stitch the motif on a solid color sweater that
looks good with the colors of the vegetables.

Use two strands of same weight yarn as sweater or
an equivalent amount of embroidery floss.

(Chart is on page 78.)

KEY TO CHART

·	= light beige
╱	= dark beige
═	= dark gray green
⬙	= middle gray green
│	= light gray green
⊓	= blue green
▼	= bright green
⊘	= green
■	= dark green
⠿	= gray green
☐	= white
X	= ecru
▷	= light pink
╱	= sand
⠐	= khaki
▪	= dark gray brown
Z	= dark orange
◥	= light orange
⊙	= light red
◢	= red
◣	= eggplant
▼	= dark red
⠂	= lilac
S	= dark lilac
●	= purple
+	= light yellow
⊠	= ochre
⌐	= yellow
○	= brick

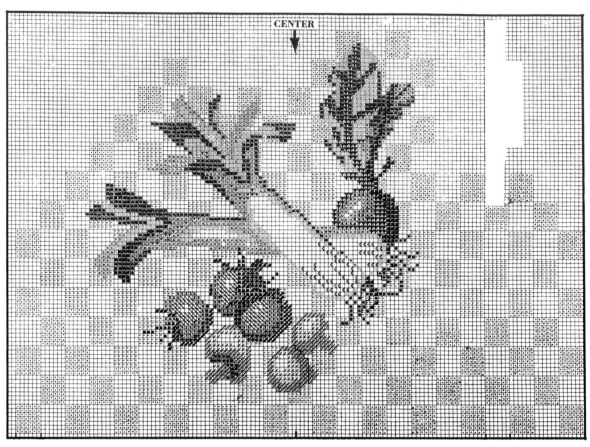

VEGETABLE MEDLEY I

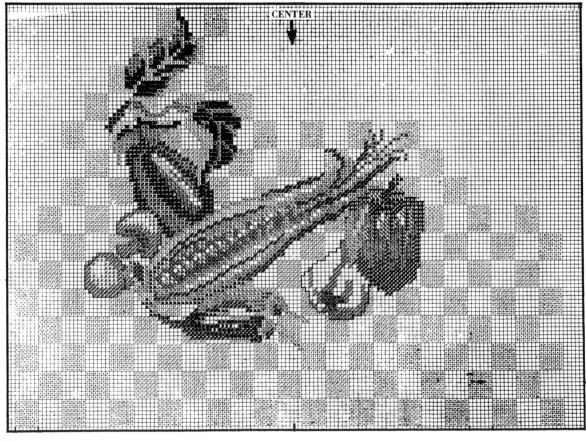

VEGETABLE MEDLEY II

STRAWBERRY

THIS JUMBO STRAWBERRY MAKES AN APPETIZING
AND FUN DESIGN ON A SUNNY YELLOW SWEATER.

Intermediate

Medium Gauge

Original fiber used: Cotton

Gauge: 18 sts x 21 rows

Size of motif: 44 sts x 55 rows

Center chart on the back or front of the sweater.

Use one strand of same weight yarn as sweater.

↑
CENTER

KEY TO CHART

☐ = yellow (background color)

⊘ = red

◢ = green

Seashore/
Summer

SHRIMP FIESTA

THIS FUN PULLOVER IS AS INVITING AND EYE-PLEASING AS FRESH SHRIMP COCKTAIL (SORRY, SHRIMP!).

Intermediate

Medium Gauge

Original fiber used: Cotton

Gauge: 19 sts x 24 rows

Size of motif: 26 sts x 30 rows

Scatter motifs on front, back and sleeves of sweater. Turn chart upside down to reverse motif and sideways to vary the design.

Use two lengths of six-strand embroidery floss.

KEY TO CHART

- ⊡ = white
- ⁘ = light salmon
- ☒ = medium salmon
- ◪ = dark salmon
- ■ = black
- _ = orange in stem stitch

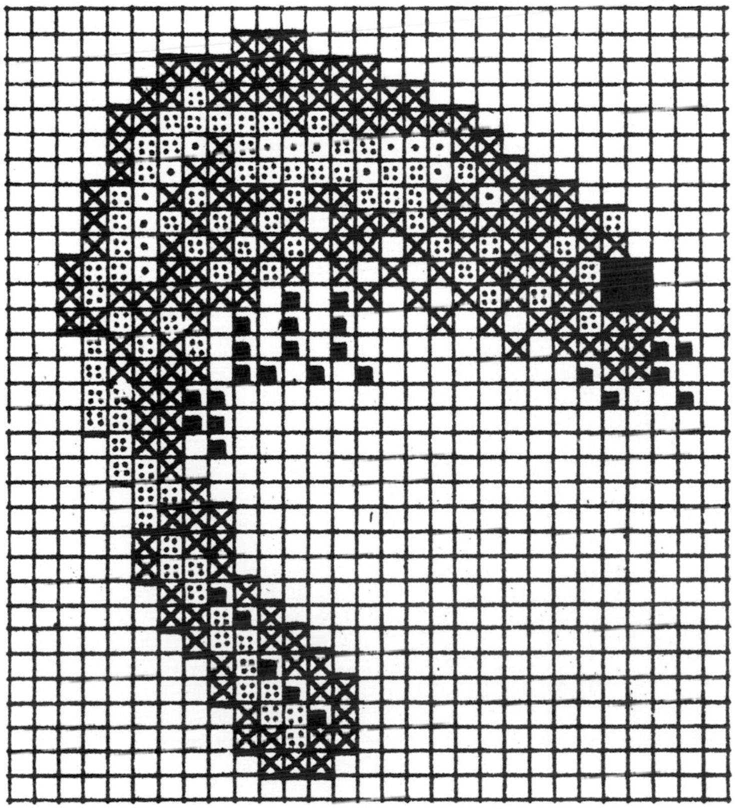

SEASHELLS

SEASHELLS DECORATE THIS PRETTY SWEATER AS NATURALLY AS THEY DO ON A SUMMER BEACH.

Intermediate

Medium Gauge

Original fiber used: Cotton

Gauge: 19 sts x 24 rows

Size of motif: 27 sts x 23 rows

Scatter motifs on front, back and sleeves of sweater. Turn chart upside down to reverse motif and sideways to vary the design.

Use two lengths of six-strand embroidery floss for each color.

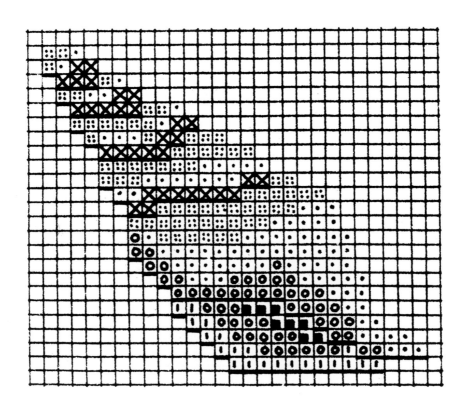

LONE BOAT

THESE CHARMING SAILBOATS HAVE
SUCH SIMPLE LINES THAT THE MOTIF
RESEMBLES AN ABSTRACT PATTERN.

Intermediate

Large Gauge

Original fiber used: Wool

Gauge: 17 sts x 24 rows

Size of child's motif: 43 sts x 46 rows

Size of teen's motif: 55 x 55

Center chart on the front of each sweater. The
woman's motif is more detailed than the child's.

Use one strand of same weight yarn as sweater.

(Charts are on page 86.)

Lone Boat

CHILD'S MOTIF

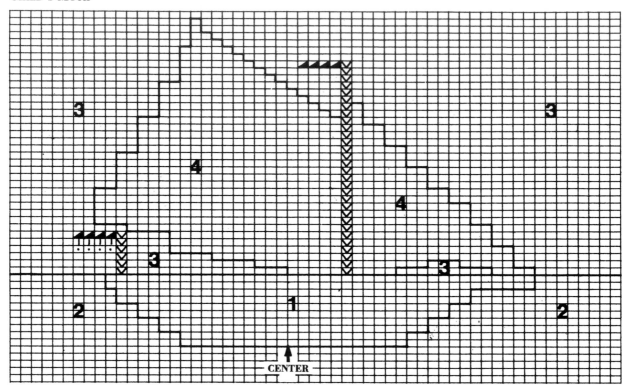

TEEN'S MOTIF

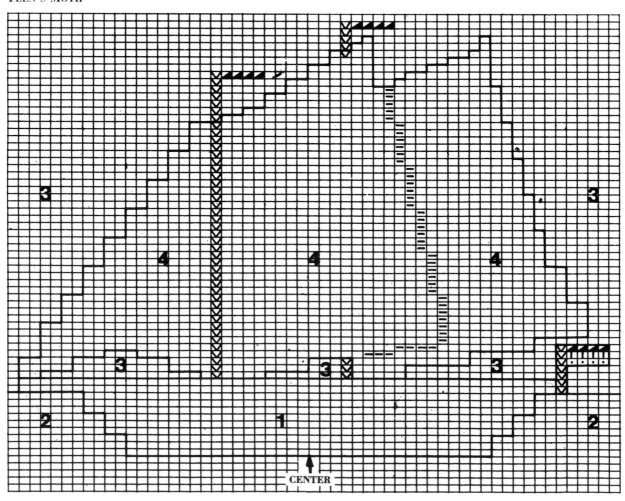

BEACH MAGIC

THIS ADORABLE CHILD'S SWEATER FEATURES A COLORFUL
PATCHWORK OF TIMELESS BEACH IMAGES.

(Charts are on pages 88 and 89.)

Intermediate

Fine Gauge

Original fiber used: Cotton

Gauge: 24 sts x 34 rows

Size of motif: 68 sts x 80 rows

Center each chart on the front and back of sweater. If motif is done on a solid color sweater, use lines on chart as a guide, and duplicate stitch to outline squares. Or, you can scatter the different patterns all over a sweater for an equally interesting effect.

Use one strand of same weight yarn as sweater.

CENTER

FRONT CHART

88

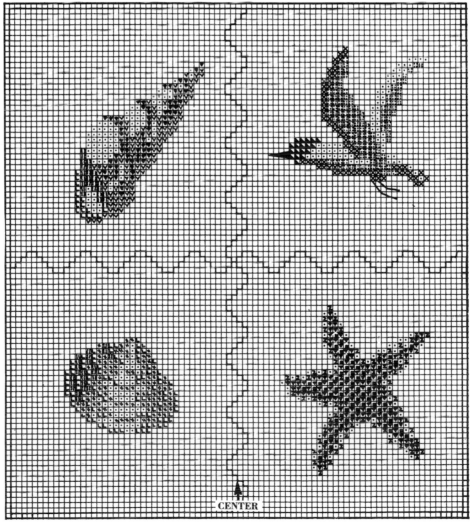

BACK CHART

SEAHORSE

THIS CRISP LOOKING SWEATER IS SURE TO PLEASE
ANY BEACHCOMBER, LARGE OR SMALL.

Intermediate

Medium Gauge

Original fiber used: Cotton

Gauge: 19 sts x 28 rows

Size of small motif: 49 sts x 55 rows

Size of large motif: 72 sts x 110 rows

Center large chart on the front of larger size sweaters. Center small chart on the front of smaller size sweaters. Motifs can be used separately or together as shown.

Use one strand of same weight yarn as sweater.

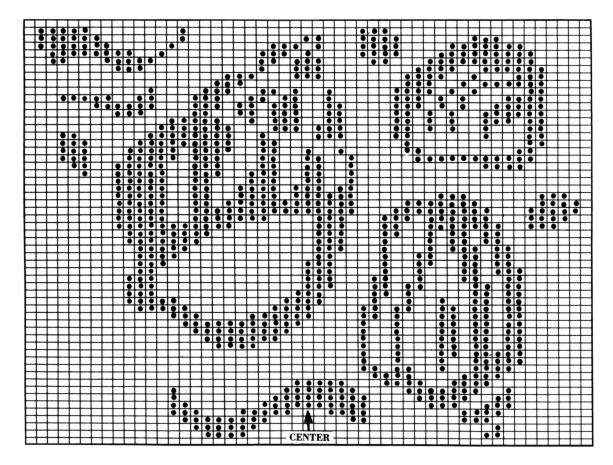

CENTER

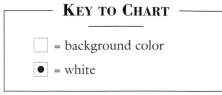

KEY TO CHART

☐ = background color

● = white

(Large chart is on page 92.)

Seashore

CENTER

Seagulls

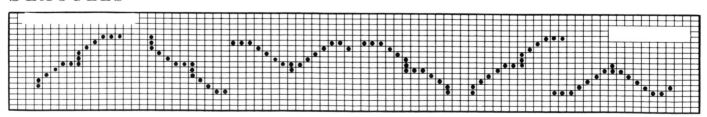

SEAGULLS

A FLOCK OF SEAGULLS, DEPICTED IN AN ABSTRACT STYLE,
HAPPILY SOAR ALL OVER THIS SUMMER-COLORED SWEATER.

Simple

Medium Gauge

Original fiber used: Cotton

Gauge: 19 sts x 26 rows

Size of motif: 78 sts x 11 rows

Center each chart on the front
and back of sweater. This simple
motif can be worked in any color
as often as you desire.

Use one strand of same weight
yarn as sweater.

KEY TO CHART

☐ = background color

● = red or blue

(Chart is on page 92.)

TWIN SAILBOATS

THIS MOTIF IS SURE TO PLEASE YOUNG SAILORS EAGER TO FEEL OCEAN WINDS AND ROLLING WAVES.

Intermediate

Medium Gauge

Original fiber used: Cotton

Gauge: 19 sts x 26 rows

Size of small motif: 47 sts x 53 rows

Size of large motif: 55 sts x 65 rows

Center large chart on front of larger size sweater.
Center small chart on front of smaller size sweater.
This design works best on a blue-striped sweater.

Use one strand of same weight yarn as sweater.

KEY TO CHARTS

☐ = blue (background color)

◹ = red

⊟ = white

◤ = gray

◨ = dark blue

— = dark gray in stem stitch

(Charts are on page 96.)

94

TWIN SAILBOATS

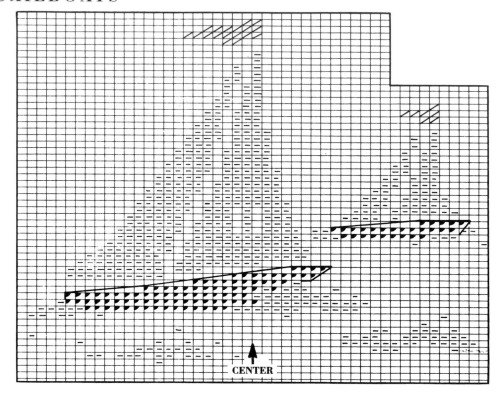

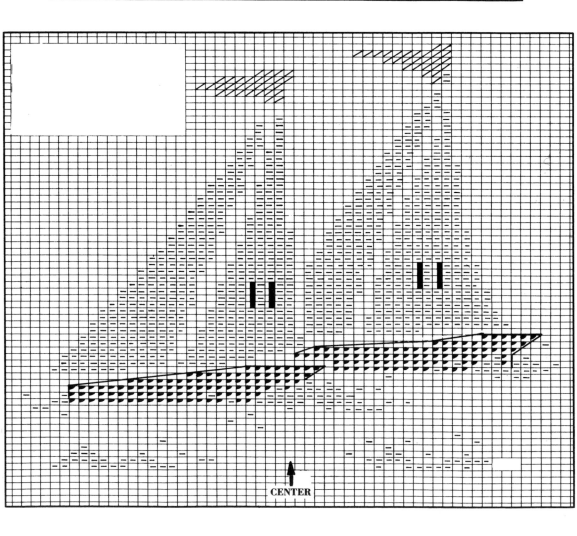

REINDEER

A FRIENDLY REINDEER AND A TOUCH OF PINK
SWEETEN UP THIS TOASTY-WARM GIRL'S SWEATER.

(Photo on preceeding page)

Simple

Large Gauge

Original fiber used: Wool

Gauge: 12.5 sts x 16 rows

Size of motif: 49 sts x 64 rows

Center chart on the front of the
sweater. The simple graphic motif
works great on bulky knits.

Use one strand of same weight
yarn as sweater.

KEY TO CHART

☐ = brown (background color)

⊙ = pink

☒ = white

REPEAT

CENTER

WINTER HEARTS

HERE'S A WINTER BEAUTY OF A SWEATER THAT LETS YOU WEAR A STRING
OF HEARTS ON YOUR SLEEVE (AND ANYWHERE ELSE YOU'D LIKE).

Intermediate

Large Gauge

Original fiber used: Wool

Gauge: 12 sts x 17 rows

Size of motif: 34 sts x 27 rows

Center chart across front and back at armhole
level and at top of sleeves. Chart also could be
used along lower edge of body and sleeves.

Use one strand of same weight yarn as sweater.

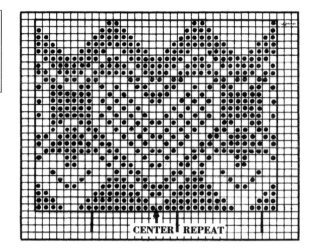

KEY TO CHART

● = red (background color)

☐ = white

CENTER REPEAT

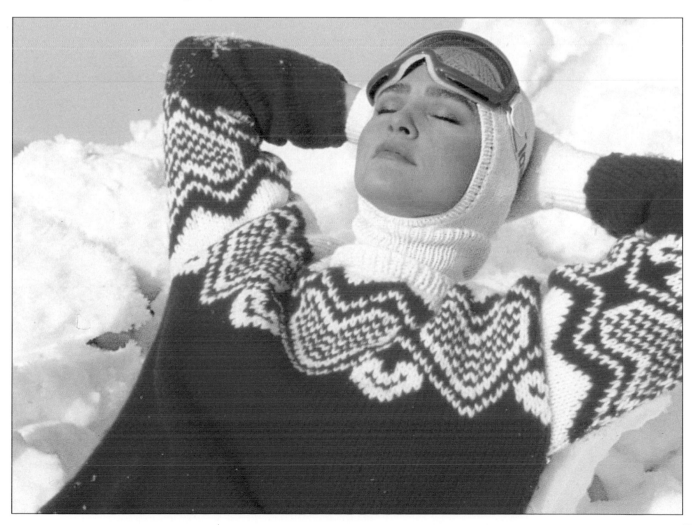

POLAR BEARS

TWIN POLAR BEARS ROAM THROUGH A MAZE MOTIF THAT
IS AS INTRICATE AND BEAUTIFUL AS A SNOWFLAKE.

Complex

Large Gauge

Original fiber used: Wool

Gauge: 12 sts x 15 rows

Size of motif: 78 sts x 95 rows

Center chart on the back and front of the sweater.
It is not necessary to embroider the entire motif.
For a much easier sweater, start at point A and
embroider only the bear motif.

Use one strand of same weight yarn as sweater.

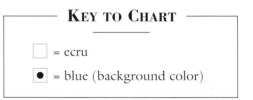

KEY TO CHART

☐ = ecru

● = blue (background color)

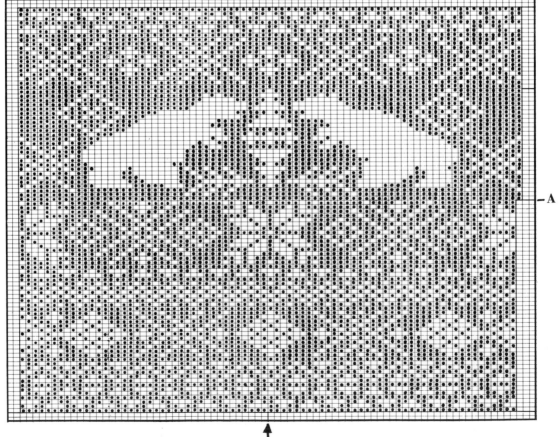

CENTER

CRYSTAL DIAMONDS

THE DIAMOND MOTIF ON THIS SPORTY SWEATER PERFECTLY
ECHOES THE SPIRIT OF OUTDOOR WINTER FUN.

Intermediate

Medium Gauge

Original fiber used: Wool

Gauge: 19 sts x 26 rows

Size of motif: 118 sts x 138 rows

Center chart on the back, front
and sleeves of the sweater. Each
diamond motif is slightly different.
If an all-over design is not desired,
pick any of the diamonds and
work a stripe of diamonds above
the armholes.

Use one strand of same weight
yarn as sweater.

CENTER

KEY TO CHART

☐ = gray (background color)

⊟ = red

⊠ = ecru

◪ = black

103

SNOWFLAKES

DRAMATIC BLACK SNOWFLAKES AND BOLD RED DOTS STAND OUT
BEAUTIFULLY AGAINST A WHITE BACKGROUND.

Intermediate

Medium Gauge

Original fiber used: Wool

Gauge: 19 sts x 25 rows

Size of motif: 52 sts x 136 rows

Center chart on the back, front and sleeves of the
sweater. The snowflake motifs can be used separately or in this completely covered rendition.

Use one strand of same weight yarn as sweater.

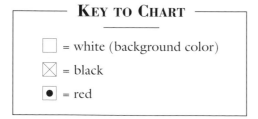

KEY TO CHART

☐ = white (background color)

☒ = black

● = red

CENTER

ICICLES

COOL-COLORED TRIANGLES ON A LONG TURTLENECK
IMITATE ICICLES AND SNOW-COVERED MOUNTAIN PEAKS.

Intermediate

Large Gauge

Original fiber used: Wool

Gauge: 15 sts x 17 rows

Size of motif: 32 sts x 58 rows

Center chart on the back, front and sleeves of the
sweater. The beauty of the design comes from the
change in background color. Motif will work well
on any sweater with two colors on the front. For
an entirely different effect, duplicate stitch on a
solid background.

Use one strand of same weight yarn as sweater.

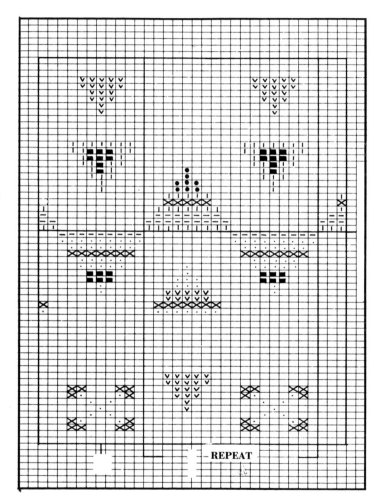

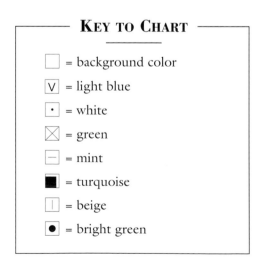

KEY TO CHART

☐ = background color

V = light blue

• = white

⊠ = green

– = mint

■ = turquoise

❘ = beige

● = bright green

CHRISTMAS COLORS

THIS SWEATER OWES ITS APPEAL TO A STRIKING STRIPED BACKGROUND
THAT EMPHASIZES THE FAMILIAR COLORS OF CHRISTMAS.

CHART FOR GREEN MOTIF

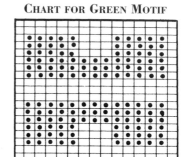

Simple

Large Gauge

Original fiber used: Wool

Gauge: 12 sts x 17 rows

Size of red motif: 10 sts x 13 rows

Size of green motif: 13 sts x 15 rows

Embroider on a striped sweater, and alternate red
and green motifs in pairs. Motif also will work well
on a one-color sweater.

Use one strand of same weight yarn as sweater.

KEY TO CHARTS

☐ = background color

▧ = red

● = green

CHART FOR RED MOTIF

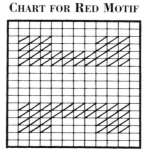

PAW PRINTS

ALTHOUGH THE DOG'S FACE IS ADORABLE, IT'S THE PAW
PRINTS THAT LEAVE A LASTING AND WINNING IMPRESSION.

(Photo on preceeding page)

Intermediate

Fine Gauge

Original fiber used: Wool

Gauge: 24 sts x 31 rows

Size of large motif: 58 sts x 71 rows

Size of small motif: 9 sts x 13 rows

Center large chart on the front of the sweater.
Scatter the small motif on back and sleeves.

Use one strand of same weight yarn as sweater.
For puppy face and paws, use a boucle yarn.

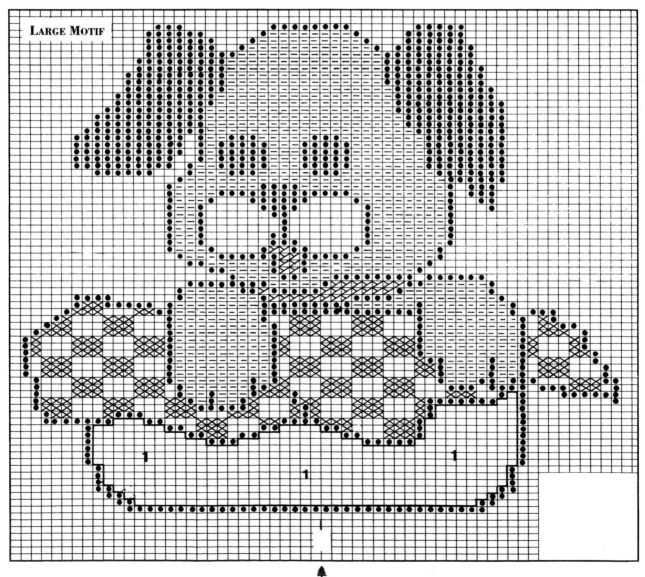

LARGE MOTIF

CENTER

KEY TO CHARTS

● = black

☒ = and 1 = blue

☐ = white (background color)

⊟ – white boucle

⊠ = red

SMALL MOTIF

PUPPY POCKET

WHAT CHILD WOULDN'T LOVE TO HAVE A CUTE PUPPY
PEEKING OUT OF HER POCKET?

POCKET MOTIF

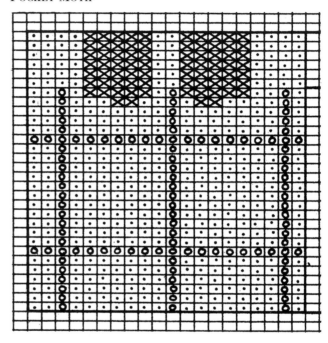

Simple

Fine Gauge

Original fiber used: Cotton

Gauge: 24 sts x 35 rows

Size of dog motif: 20 sts x 21 rows

Size of pocket motif: 20 sts x 30 rows

Place the dog motif on right front above a pocket.
Embroider the pocket following chart. The dog
motif can be used with or without the pocket
motif.

Use one strand of same weight yarn as sweater.

DOG MOTIF

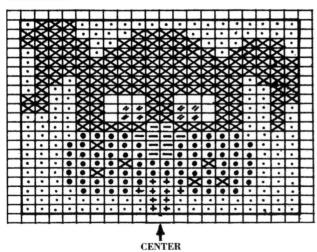

CENTER

KEY TO CHARTS

☐ = ecru

· = yellow (background color)

☒ = gray

⊙ = light green

⊟ = light pink

⊞ = bright pink

⊘ = light blue/green

⬤ = black

112

TEDDY BEAR AND FLOWERS

THE EVER-POPULAR TEDDY BEAR IS PORTRAYED
AGAINST A BACKGROUND OF COLORFUL FLOWERS.

Complex

Fine Gauge

Original fiber used: Cotton

Gauge: 27 sts x 36 rows

Size of large motif: 63 sts x 88 rows

Size of small motif (one repeat): 35 sts x 17 rows

Center teddy bear on the front of sweater. Embroider
border motif above ribbing on back and front.

The original sweater varied the number of strands of
embroidery floss from one to four strands to give depth
to the design. Be sure to use indicated number of strands.

KEY TO CHARTS

- ☐ = background color
- ╱ = light moss green - 3 strands
- ⊠ = moss green - 4 strands
- ◖ = dark pink - 2 strands
- ⌓ = pink - 1 strand
- · = light blue - 1 strand
- ⌐ = blue - 1 strand
- Z = brown - 1 strand
- ⊙ = rust - 2 strands
- ~ = yellow - 2 strands
- ■ = dark gray - 1 strand

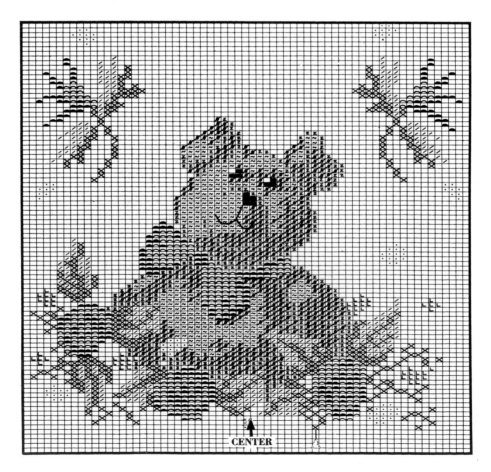

CENTER

TEDDY BEAR AND PUPPY

MR. TEDDY BEAR AND HIS PUPPY FRIEND STEAL
THE SHOW ON THIS PRECIOUS BABY PULLOVER.

KEY TO CHART

5 = light blue (background color)

● = brown

— and 6 = light yellow

V and 7 = ochre

⊠ = mint

• and 8 = light mint

☐ and 9 = pink

L = dark pink

■ = black

◹ = ecru

Intermediate

Very Fine Gauge

Original fiber used: Cotton

Gauge: 26 sts x 38 rows

Size of motif: 86 sts x 107 rows

Center chart on the front of the sweater.

Use one strand of same weight yarn as sweater.

CENTER

DOLPHIN

A LEAPING DOLPHIN AND THE COLORS OF THE SEA
BRING THIS SUMMER SWEATER TO LIFE.

KEY TO CHART

☐ = light turquoise (background color)

● = dark blue

╱ = white

− = medium blue

▮ = black

Intermediate

Medium Gauge

Original fiber used: Cotton

Gauge: 19 sts x 26 rows

Size of motif: 67 sts x 75 rows

Center chart on the front of the sweater. This design is best worked on a turquoise sweater.

Use one strand of same weight yarn as sweater.

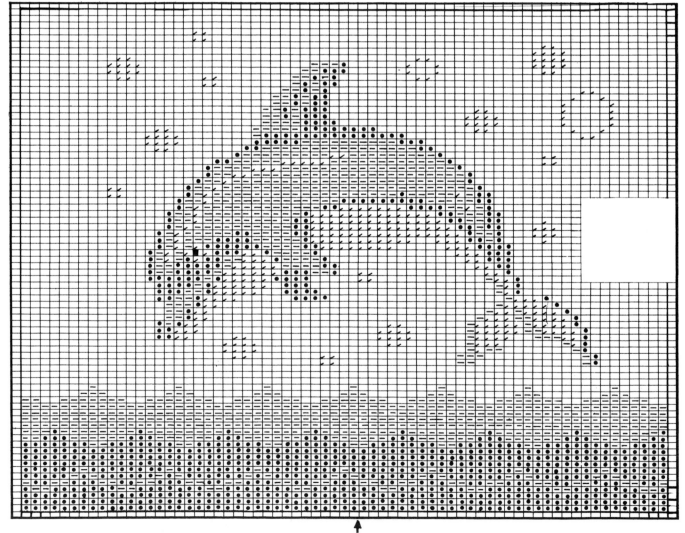

CENTER

BEAR CLOWNS

A PAIR OF BEARS, BOUNCING WITH COLOR, ARE GIVEN
A STYLIZED LOOK IN THIS PAIR OF PULLOVERS.

Intermediate

Medium Gauge

Original fiber used: Cotton

Gauge: 19 sts x 25 rows

Size of large motif: 42 sts x 50 rows

Size of smaller motif: 36 sts x 41 rows

Center chart on the front of the sweater. Choose
Chart 1 or Chart 2 based on the size of sweater to
be embroidered. This is a good motif to use on a
raglan sleeve sweater.

Use one strand of same weight yarn as sweater.

CHART 1

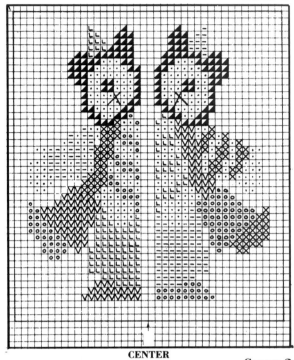

CENTER

CHART 2

CENTER

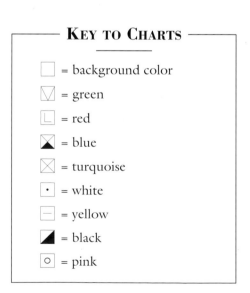

KEY TO CHARTS

☐ = background color

▽ = green

L = red

◣ = blue

⊠ = turquoise

· = white

— = yellow

◢ = black

○ = pink

MONKEY

THIS PRECIOUS BABY'S SWEATER DELIVERS
JUST THE RIGHT AMOUNT OF MONKEY BUSINESS.

KEY TO CHARTS

☐ – white (background color)

⊞ and 7 = blue

⊡ and 8 = ecru

◢ = black

◹ and 9 = ochre

⊙ = brown

◢ = red

⊠ = gray

⊟ = pink

Ⅴ – light green

⊙ = green

Complex

Fine Gauge

Original fiber used: Wool

Gauge: 22 sts x 30 rows

Size of large motif: 72 sts x 102 rows

Size of small motif: 33 sts x 52 rows

Center large motif on front. Optional: Scatter
flower, triangle and dot motifs on sleeves; (small
chart shows these designs).

Use one strand of same weight yarn as sweater.

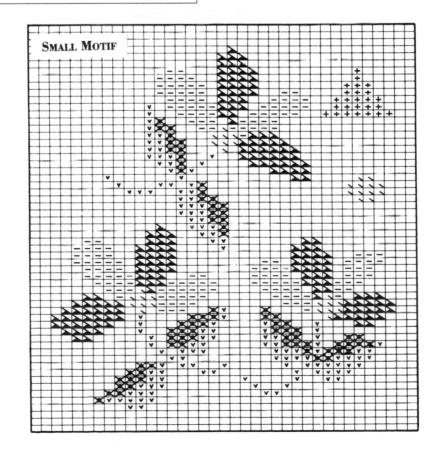

SMALL MOTIF

*(Monkey chart is
on page 127.)*

FISH DINNER

THE CATCH OF THE DAY MOTIF ON THIS COLORFUL SWEATER
IS DEFINITELY THE CAT'S MEOW.

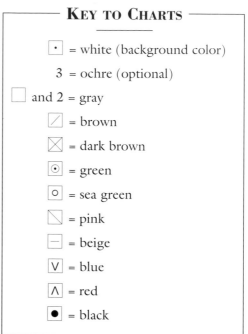

KEY TO CHARTS

- · = white (background color)
- 3 = ochre (optional)
- ☐ and 2 = gray
- ⧄ = brown
- ⧅ = dark brown
- ⊙ = green
- ○ = sea green
- ⬓ = pink
- ⊟ = beige
- V = blue
- Λ = red
- ● = black

Complex

Fine Gauge

Original fiber used: Cotton

Gauge: 23 sts x 30 rows

Size of motif: 84 sts x 81 rows

Center chart on the front of the sweater. For extra
fun, center the other chart on the back of the
sweater.

Use one strand of same weight yarn as sweater.

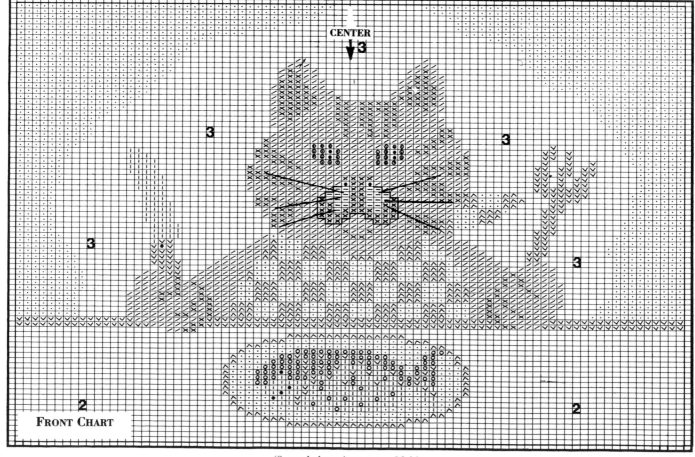

CENTER
↓3

3   3

3

3

3

2   2

FRONT CHART

(Second chart is on page 126.)

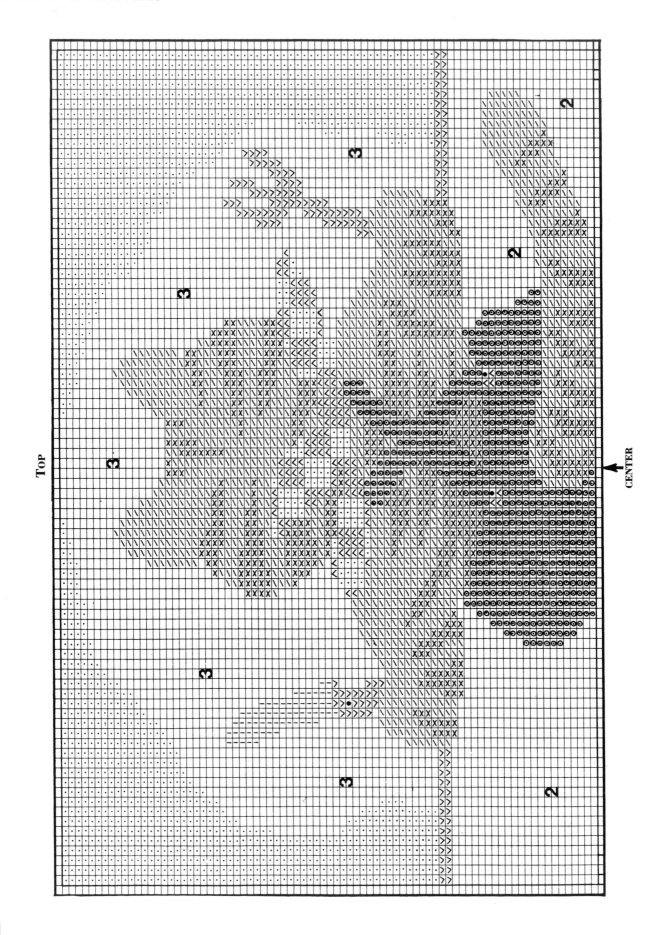

MONKEY

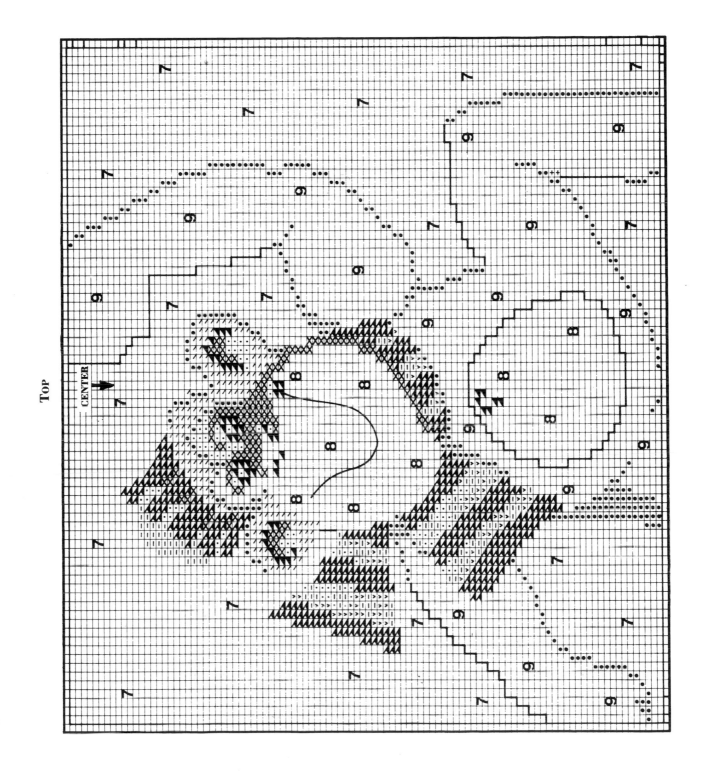

INDEX